# 250 Ketogenic Fat Bombs

*The Big Book of Sweet*
*and Savory Snacks*
*(Extra Fat Bomb Dip Recipes)*

**Gloria Lee**

Disclaimer:

This book is intended for entertainment and information purposes only. The author and any other creators of this book are in no way liable or hold any responsibility for the adverse effects that you may take from directly or indirectly reading this book. It's advised that you seek a medical professional if you plan on altering your diet or taking up any health related practice.

# Table of Contents

# Introduction

Thank you for taking the time grab ahold of my book: 250 Ketogenic Fat Bombs - The Big Book of Sweet & Savory Snacks.

This book contains 250 simple ketogenic fat bombs recipes and 6 tasty dip recipes to compliment the fat bombs that you'll eat. You will also develop a deeper understanding of what the ketogenic diet is and what it is that makes a fat bomb.

Make sure to keep this cookbook at your fingertips as it's a great book to come back to when you are in desperation for a new yummy fat bomb recipe. With 250 recipes at your disposal, you will never get sick of eating the same fat bombs over and over again!

I hope you greatly enjoy this cookbook, and if you find these recipes delicious, then please leave a review for my book on Amazon.

# The Ketogenic Diet and Fat Bombs Explained

Once upon a time, when humans were hunters and gatherers, they needed something besides carbohydrates to create energy when certain types of foods were not available. Over time, the liver developed the ability to produce what are known as ketones to create energy when carbohydrates are not available. While the liver still possesses this ability, the ease with which glucose (found in high amounts in carbs) is broken down into energy, coupled with the amount of carbohydrates in the average diet, means that the liver rarely has a chance to shine.

The ketogenic diet aims to change this by removing a majority of the carbohydrates the body can break down on a regular basis. This in turn brings on what is known as a state of ketosis whereby the liver uses up excess fat (promoting weight loss) to create the energy no longer being provided by the carbohydrates.

While ketosis can be brought on by consuming significantly fewer calories than normal, it turns out that cutting out most carbohydrates tricks the body into the same mode. When it comes to limiting your carbohydrates, a good guideline to shoot for is to consume less than 15 net carb grams per day. To determine your net carbs, you simply add up how many carbohydrates you consumed in a 24-hour period and then subtract that number from the amount of fiber you consumed during that same amount of time.

Prior to making any major dietary changes you should always consult a healthcare professional or registered nutritionist to ensure that you aren't accidentally doing more harm to yourself then good. When it comes to sticking to the ketogenic diet, net carbohydrates should only make up 5 percent of your diet, 25 percent should be protein and the remaining 70 percent should be made up of healthy fats. Wheats and starches of all types should be off limits and most carbohydrates should come from nuts, vegetables and dairy products.

Dark, leafy green vegetables should be a staple of most meals as should several natural fats and a good source of protein. Consider meals such as chicken with vegetables coated with olive oil, or steak with roasted cauliflower slathered in butter. If you need to snack, reach for things healthy, some great fatty options such as seeds, nuts, peanut butter or cheeses are welcomed on the ketogenic diet. Despite the fact that fats have received a bad rap in the media, without carbohydrates holding you back, you will find that fats are far more useful than you have been led to believe.

**Reasons to give the ketogenic diet a try**

- Start feeling full more quickly and feel full longer: Fats and protein are more filling and therefore you will be satisfied with your meal longer than products which are filled with carbohydrates.

- Targeted fat removal: Ketosis targets what is known as visceral fat first and foremost. This is great news for almost everyone as visceral fat is the fat that is stored around the midsection.

- Cut down your chance of heart disease: The triglycerides that are found in large amount in carbohydrates are also found in high concentrations in those who have experienced cardiovascular problems.

- Promote good cholesterol: Seeds and nuts are high in fats, which is great when you need a quick burst of energy, but they are also rich in HDL, a positive type of cholesterol.

**Utilizing Fat Bombs**

Once you have made the decision to cut almost all of the carbohydrates from your diet, you'll need to come up with additional ways to feel full and gain energy between meals. This is where fat bombs come in; fat bombs are quick and easy to eat snacks that are typically made from a small number of sweet or savory ingredients. Fat bombs can also include foods such as; seeds, nuts, coconut oil and butter, which are the healthy fats that your body is now relying upon.

These concentrated energy snacks will quickly fill you up and prevent you from breaking down during the day. But, best of all, fat bombs are so tasty that you will never feel tempted to reach for something that's been processed and packed full of carbohydrates. Fat bombs are a great choice before the gym or when you are struggling to make it from lunch all the way to dinner. Plus, getting the required amount of fat in your diet every day can be more difficult than it first appears. Remember, it is important to always stick to healthy fats otherwise you are just binging on items that have little true nutritional value.

Fat Bomb precautions: Like any other new dietary supplement, when you first begin trying out different fat bomb recipes it is important to do so cautiously at first as you never know how your body might respond. As previously discussed, it's likely that your body hasn't regularly consumed this much healthy fat before, it may take a little while to accept the change. However, if you keep at it you should find that you have adapted to the change relatively quickly. It is important to consume fat bombs in moderation as relying on them too heavily can cause a dependence to form. They should be a small part of your daily ketogenic diet, not a core pillar. Use discretion if you find yourself eating more than 2 per day.

Fat bomb creation basics: Yes, this is a cookbook that contains 250 fat bomb recipes, so you may not care too much about creating your own unique fat bombs. However, if you do which to understand the process behind the creation of the fat bomb, read this short section mentioned below...

Fat bombs are a great addition to a low carbohydrate and protein diet as they are typically based either around satisfying cravings you might have for either sweet or savory foods. What's more, they are infinitely malleable as the only requirement is lots of healthy fats, the rest is up for you.

When it comes to making your own fat bomb recipes, it is important to shoot for an item that is high in fat, this will ensure your bombs are as effective as possible. Typically, fat bombs contain only a few ingredients, generally they start with a base of healthy fat, typically a coconut derivative, grass-fed butter or cream cheese, still other fat bombs can vary. Some type of flavoring and an additional ingredient or two is usually added to the fat bomb.

As a rule, coconut oil is the healthiest option when it comes to choosing a base fat. It is the type of fat that burns the quickest, and, once your body reaches ketosis, it is turned into energy practically as soon as it is absorbed by your body.

# *Fat Bomb Recipes*

## 1. Bacon and Cilantro Bombs

**Time taken:** 30 minutes
(plus 25 minutes chilling time)
**Servings:** 6

### Ingredients:

- 2 large organic eggs
- 1/4 cup butter, salted
- 2 tbsp organic mayonnaise
- 1/4 cup fresh cilantro, chopped
- 1/4 tsp freshly ground pepper
- 1/4 tsp salt, to taste
- 5 slices bacon

### Directions:

1. Preheat the oven to 190C/375F.
2. Line a baking pan with wax paper and lay the strips of bacon on it.
3. Let it cook in the oven for 12-15 minutes, until crisp.
4. While the bacon is in the oven, using a small pot, boil the eggs.
5. Add a pinch of salt to the water and let boil for about 12 minutes.
6. When the bacon is done, take it out of the oven, let it cool for a couple of minutes and chop it into tiny bits.
7. Once the eggs are cooked, remove the hot water and replace it with cool water. Let eggs cool down and peel the shells off.
8. In a small bowl, mash the eggs with a fork.
9. Add the butter and mash together.
10. Add the mayonnaise and season with a little bit of salt and pepper.
11. Add the cilantro and mix well.
12. Cover the bowl with cling wrap and let it sit in the fridge for 25 minutes, or until it firms up.
13. Remove the bowl from the fridge and roll egg mixture into small balls.
14. Roll the balls in the chopped bacon to coat.
15. Serve and enjoy!

# 2. Minty Avocado and Bacon Bombs

**Time taken:** 25 minutes
(plus 25 minutes chilling time)
**Servings:** 6

## Ingredients:

- 1 avocado, pitted and sliced
- 1/4 cup butter, salted
- 2 cloves garlic, minced finely
- 1 small white onion, diced finely
- 1 tbsp lemon juice
- 1/2 tsp cayenne pepper
- 1/4 tsp salt, to taste
- 2 tbsp fresh mint leaves, chopped
- 2 tbsp fresh cilantro, chopped
- 5 slices bacon

## Directions:

1. Preheat the oven to 190C/375F.
2. Line a baking pan with wax paper and lay the strips of bacon on it.
3. Let it cook in the oven for 12-15 minutes, until crisp.
4. In a bowl, mash together the avocado, butter, garlic, onions, cayenne pepper, mint leaves and cilantro with a fork.
5. Add the butter and mash together.
6. Add the lemon juice and season with a little bit of salt and pepper.
7. Cover the bowl with some cling wrap and let it sit in the fridge for 25 minutes, or until it firms up.
8. Remove the bowl from the fridge and roll the mixture into small balls.
9. Roll the balls in the chopped bacon to coat.
10. Serve and enjoy!

---

# 3. Butter Almond Bacon Bombs

**Time taken:** 25 minutes
**Servings:** 10

## Ingredients:

- 1/4 cup almonds, chopped
- 1/4 cup butter, salted
- 2 cloves garlic, minced finely
- 1/4 cup cream cheese
- 1 small white onion, diced finely
- 1/4 tsp salt, to taste
- 5 slices bacon

## Directions:

1. Preheat the oven to 190C/375F.
2. Cut the bacon strips in half or into 2 1/2 inch pieces.
3. Line a baking pan with wax paper and lay the strips of bacon on it.
4. Let it cook in the oven for 12-15 minutes until crisp.
5. In a bowl, mash the butter, garlic, onions and cream cheese together with a fork.
6. Add salt and pepper to taste
7. Lay out the bacon strips on a plate. Scoop the butter and cheese mixture onto the bacon strips.
8. Sprinkle almond bits over the butter and cheese mixture and serve. Enjoy!

# 4. Three-Cheese and Olive Fat Bombs

**Time taken:** 15 minutes
(plus 25 minutes chilling time)
**Servings:** 5

## Ingredients:

- 1/2 cup cream cheese
- 1/4 cup butter, salted, cut into small pieces
- 1 tbsp fresh basil, chopped
- 1 tbsp fresh cilantro, chopped
- 5 olives, pitted & sliced
- 2 cloves garlic, crushed
- 1 tsp pepper
- 1/4 tsp salt, to taste
- 5 tbsp fresh mozzarella cheese
- 5 tbsp parmesan cheese

## Directions:

1. In a bowl, mash together the butter, mozzarella cheese and cream cheese with a fork.
2. Add the fresh basil, cilantro, olives and garlic.
3. Add salt and pepper to taste.
4. Cover the bowl with some cling wrap, and let it sit in the fridge for 25 minutes, or until it firms up.
5. Remove the bowl from the fridge roll the mixture into small balls.
6. Roll the balls in the parmesan cheese to coat.
7. Serve and enjoy!

# 5. Sugar-Free Strawberry No-Bake Bombs

**Time taken:** 25 minutes
(plus 2 hours 30 minutes chilling time)
**Servings:** 40

## Ingredients:

- 8 ounces cream cheese, softened
- 1/2 cup stevia powder (or other sugar-free substitute)
- 2 tbsp heavy cream
- pinch salt
- 3 teaspoons strawberry extract
- 3 drops red food coloring
- 1/4 cup coconut oil
- 1 1/2 cup sugar free chocolate chips

## Directions:

1. Using an electric mixer, mix the cream cheese and stevia together until smooth.
2. Add the cream, salt, strawberry extract and red food coloring.
3. Continue mixing until thoroughly combined.
4. Slowly add in the coconut oil and continue to mixing on high, scraping down the edges of the bowl as necessary, until it's all incorporated.
5. Cover the mixture with cling wrap and chill for 1 hour.
6. Line a baking tray with wax paper.
7. Remove mixture from the fridge and using a small ice cream scoop, scoop into 40 small balls onto the baking tray.
8. Freeze the balls for 30 minutes.
9. While waiting, melt the chocolate, making sure it's not too hot to coat the balls.

10. Take the balls out of the freezer and one by one, drop them in the bowl of melted chocolate to coat. Scoop coated balls out and place them back onto the tray.

11. Chill for 1 hour or until the chocolate coating hardens.
12. Serve and enjoy!

# 6. Chocolate Coconut Candy Cups

**Time taken:** 20 minutes
(plus 55 minutes chilling time)
**Servings:** 20 cups

## Ingredients:

- Coconut candies:
- 1/2 cup coconut butter
- 1/2 cup coconut oil
- 1/2 cup desiccated coconut
- 3 tbsp stevia
- Chocolate Topping:
- 2 cups dark sugar-free chocolate

## Directions:

1. Line 20 wells of a mini-muffin pan with paper liners.
2. Combine coconut butter and coconut oil in a small saucepan.
3. Stir gently over low heat until it's all melted and smooth.
4. Add in the desiccated coconut and stevia until everything is incorporated.
5. Pour the coconut candy into the prepared muffin cups to 3/4 full and let chill for 35 minutes in the fridge, or until it firms up.
6. Melt the dark sugar-free chocolate and let it cool down a bit.
7. Pour the chocolate on top of the coconut candy.
8. Chill for another 20 minutes.
9. Serve and enjoy!

# 7. Sugar-Free Lemon Mini Tarts

**Time taken:** 20 minutes
(plus 1-2 hours chilling time)
**Servings:** 24 tarts

## Ingredients:

Crust:
- 1 cup almond meal
- 3/4 cup desiccated coconut
- 2 tbsp stevia
- 3 tbsp lemon juice
- 1 1/2 tsp vanilla

- 4 1/2 tablespoons butter, salted, melted

Filling:
- 1/2 cup butter, salted
- 1/3 cup almond milk
- 1/3 cup fresh lemon juice
- 1/4 cup stevia
- 1 tsp vanilla
- 2 tsp lemon extract
- 1 tbsp lemon zest

## Directions:

1. Line 24 wells of a mini-muffin pan with wax paper.
2. For the crusts, in a medium bowl, combine the almond meal, desiccated coconut, stevia, lemon juice, vanilla and butter.
3. Mix well and roll mixture into a long log.
4. Cut the log into 24 slices and press the slices into the wells of the muffin pan.
5. Refrigerate the crusts for 30 minutes.
6. While waiting for the crust, start making the filling.
7. Using a mixer with a whisk attachment, beat the butter until fluffy.
8. Add the almond milk, lemon juice, stevia, vanilla and lemon extract and beat until smooth.
9. Remove crusts from the fridge and pour filling into crusts.
10. Top the tarts with the lemon zest and place back in the fridge to harden.
11. Serve and enjoy!

# 8. Nutty Fudge Fat Bombs

**Time taken:** 10 minutes
(plus 30 minutes chilling time)
**Servings:** 6

## Ingredients:

- 2 oz cocoa butter
- 2 tbsp unsweetened dark chocolate powder
- 2 tbsp stevia
- 1/4 cup macadamia nuts, chopped
- 1/4 cup walnuts, chopped
- 1/4 cup chocolate chips
- 1/4 cup heavy cream

## Directions:

1. In a small double boiler, melt the cocoa butter.
2. Add the cocoa powder and stevia and mix well.
3. Add the macadamia nuts and walnuts to the mixture.
4. Slowly add the cream and mix well.
5. Pour mixture into a small square baking pan (6x6) lined with greased wax paper.
6. Sprinkle the top with the chocolate chips.
7. Put the mixture in the freezer and let it harden for 30 minutes.
8. Remove from the pan and slice to 6 portions.
9. Share and enjoy!

# 9. Chocolate Macadamia Bark

**Time taken:** 10 minutes
(plus 30 minutes chilling time)
**Servings:** 2

## Ingredients:

- 2 tbsp coconut oil
- 1 tbsp unsweetened cocoa powder
- 1 tbsp powdered sugar
- 1 tbsp macadamia nuts, chopped
- 1 tbsp heavy cream

## Directions:

1. In a small double boiler, melt the coconut oil.
2. Add cocoa powder and powdered sugar and mix well until all are incorporated.
3. Add in the chopped nuts.
4. Slowly add in the cream and stir until well combined and mixture begins to thicken.
5. Line a baking tray with wax paper. Spread bark mixture onto baking tray about 1/2 inch thick.
6. Let bark chill in the fridge for 30 minutes or until hardened.
7. Break bark in pieces and serve. Enjoy!

# 10. Nutty-Butter Squares

**Time taken:** 10 minutes
(plus 30 minutes chilling time)
**Servings:** 12

## Ingredients:

- 1 cup peanut butter
- 1/4 cup butter, salted
- 1 cup powdered sugar
- 2 tbsp heavy cream
- 1/2 tsp vanilla
- 1/4 cup walnuts, crushed

## Directions:

1. Place the peanut butter and butter in a bowl. Using a stand mixer with a paddle attachment, cream together until smooth.
2. Slowly add the powdered sugar while mixing.
3. And the cream and vanilla.
4. Add the walnuts.
5. Pour batter into a small square baking pan (6x6) lined with wax paper.
6. Place the pan in the fridge for 30 minutes or until mixture hardens.
7. Cut into equal squares, serve and enjoy!

# 11. Coconut-Ginger Bombs

**Time taken:** 10 minutes
(plus 25 minutes chilling time)
**Servings:** 10

## Ingredients:

- 1/4 cup butter, softened (salted)
- 5 tbsp coconut oil
- 3 tbsp desiccated coconut
- 1 tsp caster sugar
- 1/2 tsp ginger powder

## Directions:

1. Mix all ingredients in a bowl, making sure the sugar has completely dissolved.
2. Pour mixture into the wells of a silicone candy mold.
3. Freeze for 25 minutes or until the mixture sets and hardens.
4. Remove from the silicone mold and serve. Enjoy!

# 12. Fudge-Brownie Squares

**Time taken:** 40 minutes
**Servings:** 12 squares

## Ingredients:

- 1 cup butter, softened (salted)
- 1/3 cup heavy cream
- 1 egg
- 2 tsp vanilla
- 5 tbsp cocoa powder, sifted
- 1 cup sugar
- 1/4 tsp baking soda
- 1/4 macadamia nuts, crushed

## Directions:

1. Preheat oven to 190C/375F.
2. Using a stand mixer, cream the butter and sugar until the butter turns a light color.
3. Add the egg and vanilla and mix well until everything is incorporated.
4. Add cocoa powder, baking soda and cream slowly, making sure there are no lumps from the cocoa powder.
5. Pour batter into a greased and lined 6x6 square baking pan.
6. Sprinkle the crushed nuts on top.
7. Bake for 25-30 minutes and let cool.
8. Remove from pan and slice into 12 equal squares.
9. Serve and enjoy!

# 13. Macadamia Nut Fat Bombs

**Time taken:** 15 minutes
(plus 30-40 minutes chilling time)
**Servings:** 12 cubes

## Ingredients:

- 3/4 cup macadamia nuts
- 1/4 cup pistachios
- 1/4 cup extra virgin olive oil
- 1/4 cup butter, salted
- 2 tsp vanilla
- 3 tbsp stevia

## Directions:

1. Place the 2 kinds of nuts in the bowl of a food processor and pulse until smooth.
2. Add the butter and oil and pulse again.
3. Add the vanilla and stevia and mix until fine and smooth.
4. Pour mixture into the wells of small ice-cube trays.
5. Freeze for about 30-40 minutes.
6. Pop bombs out and serve. Enjoy!

# 14. Peppermint Fat Bombs

**Time taken:** 20 minutes
(plus 30-40 minutes chilling time)
**Servings:** 12 cubes

## Ingredients:

- 1 1/2 cup coconut oil
- 1 1/2 cup butter, unsalted
- 1/2 cup pistachios
- 1/2 cup stevia
- 2 tsp vanilla
- 1 tsp peppermint oil
- 2 drops green food coloring

## Directions:

1. Place pistachios in the bowl of a food processor and pulse until finely ground.
2. Add the butter and coconut oil and pulse again.
3. Add the vanilla and stevia and mix until fine and smooth.
4. Add the peppermint oil and the food coloring.
5. Pour the mixture into the wells of small ice-cube trays.
6. Freeze for 30-40 minutes.
7. Pop them out and serve. Enjoy!

# 15. Chocolate Pecan Fat Bombs

**Time taken:** 20 minutes (plus 2 hours chilling time)
**Servings:** 10 squares

## Ingredients:

- 1/4 cup coconut butter
- 1/2 cup coconut oil
- 4 tbsp cocoa powder
- 4 tbsp stevia
- 1/3 cup heavy cream
- 1/2 cup pecans
- 1 tsp vanilla

## Directions:

1. In a double boiler, melt coconut butter and coconut oil.
2. Whisk in the cocoa powder until smooth.
3. Pour the mixture into the bowl of a food processor and add the stevia.
4. Slowly add the cream and blend for 6-8 minutes.
5. Halfway fill wells of silicone molds with mixture.
6. Top each with pecans.
7. Pour remaining mixture into wells until full.
8. Place them in the freezer for about 2 hours.
9. Remove from the mold and serve. Enjoy!

# 16. Spicy Chocolate Fat Bombs

**Time taken:** 20 minutes (plus 2 hours chilling time)
**Servings:** 10 squares

## Ingredients:

- 1 cup heavy cream
- 2 tbsp cocoa powder
- 1 tsp vanilla
- 1 tsp cinnamon
- 1/4 tsp cayenne pepper
- 2 tbsp stevia

## Directions:

1. Heat the heavy cream in a saucepan.
2. Add the cocoa powder, vanilla, cayenne pepper, stevia and cinnamon and whisk until smooth.
3. Pour mixture into wells of an ice cube tray.
4. Freeze for about 2 hours.
5. Pop them out and serve. Enjoy!

# 17. Coconut High-Protein Fat Bombs

**Time taken:** 20 minutes
(plus 2 hours chilling time)
**Servings:** 10 squares

## Ingredients:

- 1/4 cup cacao butter
- 1 1/4 cup coconut milk
- 1/2 cup coconut oil
- 1/2 cup protein powder
- 1 tsp vanilla
- 2 tsp stevia

## Directions:

1. Melt the cacao butter in a double boiler over low heat.
2. Stir in the coconut milk and coconut oil.
3. Add the protein powder, remove from the heat and stir until smooth.
4. Add the stevia and vanilla and stir until completely incorporated.
5. Pour mixture into a lined and greased 6x6 pan.
6. Place the mixture in the freezer for 2 hours.
7. When it has hardened, remove from the pan and cut into 10 squares.
8. Serve and enjoy!

# 18. Spiced Cinnamon Fat Bombs

**Time taken:** 20 minutes
(plus 1 hour 30 minutes chilling time)
**Servings:** 10

## Ingredients:

- 1 cup coconut butter
- 1 cup coconut milk
- 1/2 tsp cinnamon
- 1/4 tsp cayenne pepper
- 1 tsp vanilla
- 1 tsp stevia
- 2 tbsp honey
- 1 cup desiccated coconut

## Directions:

1. In a double boiler, melt the coconut butter.
2. Add coconut milk, cinnamon and cayenne pepper and stir well.
3. Add the vanilla, stevia and honey and stir until everything is incorporated.
4. Pour mixture into a bowl.
5. Cover the bowl with some cling wrap and let it sit in the fridge for 30 minutes, or until it firms up.
6. Remove the bowl from the fridge and roll mixture into small balls.
7. Roll balls in the desiccated coconut to coat.
8. Refrigerate balls for 1 hour. Serve and enjoy!

# 19. Spiced Cookie Fat Bombs

**Time taken:** 20 minutes
(plus 1 hour 40 minutes chilling time)
**Servings:** 10

## Ingredients:

- 1/3 cup chocolate protein powder
- 2 tbsp coconut flour
- 2 tbsp desiccated coconut
- 4 tbsp coconut milk
- 1 tbsp cocoa powder
- 1 tsp cinnamon
- 1 tsp ginger powder
- 1 tbsp chocolate chips
- 2 tbsp crushed Oreo cookies
- 3/4 cup white chocolate

## Directions:

1. In a large bowl, mix the protein powder, coconut flour, cinnamon, ginger powder, desiccated coconut and cocoa powder.
2. Add the coconut milk and mix well
3. Add the chocolate chips and mix well.
4. Cover the bowl with some cling wrap and let it sit in the fridge for 30 minutes, or until it firms up.
5. Remove the bowl from the fridge and roll mixture into small balls.
6. Line a baking sheet with parchment paper.
7. Place the balls on the baking sheet and freeze for 10 minutes.
8. Melt the white chocolate.
9. Remove the balls from the freezer and one by one coat with white chocolate.
10. Sprinkle a little of the crushed Oreo cookies on top.
11. Place balls in the fridge for 1 hour to set.
12. Serve and enjoy!

# 20. Strawberry-Mint Cheesecake Fat Bombs

**Time taken:** 20 minutes
(plus 30 minutes chilling)
**Servings:** 12

## Ingredients:

- 3/4 cup fresh strawberries, chopped
- 3/4 cup cream cheese, softened
- 1 tbsp heavy cream
- 1/4 cup butter, unsalted softened
- 2 tbsp stevia
- 1 tbsp vanilla
- 1/4 tsp peppermint oil
- 2 tbsp crushed graham crackers

## Directions:

1. Using a stand mixer, cream the butter and cream cheese together.
2. Add the stevia, heavy cream, peppermint oil and vanilla and mix until smooth.
3. Add the chopped strawberries and mix until smooth.
4. Transfer mixture to another bowl.
5. Cover the bowl with some cling wrap and let it sit in the fridge for 30 minutes, or until it firms up.
6. Remove the bowl from the fridge and roll mixture into small balls.
7. Roll the balls in the crushed graham crackers.
8. Serve and enjoy!

# 21. Choco-Candied Almond Bark

**Time taken:** 20 minutes
(plus 1 hour chilling time)
**Servings:** 20 pieces

## Ingredients:

- 1/2 cup stevia
- 2 tbsp water
- 1 tbsp butter, melted
- 1 1/2 cups almond flakes, chopped and toasted
- 5 bacon strips, chopped and cooked until crisp
- 1/4 tsp Himalayan salt
- 1 tbsp cocoa butter, melted
- 3/4 cup dark chocolate chips, chopped, melted

## Directions:

1. Over medium heat, combine stevia and water in a medium saucepan.
2. Heat mixture to a boil, stirring occasionally, and cook until mixture darkens.
3. Remove from heat and whisk in the butter and cocoa buter.
4. Add almond flakes, bacon, salt and chocolate chips, stir quickly to coat.
5. Pour almond flake mixture onto a baking sheet lined with wax paper and add to the freezer for 1 hour.
6. Break into pieces and serve. Enjoy!

# 22. Raspberry Macadamia Cups

**Time taken:** 20 minutes (1 hour chilling)
**Servings:** 20 pieces

## Ingredients:

- 1 cup dark chocolate chips
- 1/4 cup cocoa butter
- 2 tbsp coconut oil
- 1 tsp vanilla
- 1 1/2 cup fresh raspberries
- 1/2 cup macadamia nuts

## Directions:

1. Combine dark chocolate chips and cocoa butter in a double boiler over medium heat.
2. Stir in the coconut oil and vanilla and remove from heat.
3. Line 20 wells of a mini-muffin pan with wax paper and fill each half full.
4. Put a raspberry and some macadamia nuts in each cup.
5. Pour in the rest of the mixture to fill the cups.
6. Freeze for 1 hour.
7. Serve and enjoy!

# 23. Blueberry Cream Cheese Bombs

**Time taken:** 20 minutes
(plus 1 hour chilling)
**Servings:** 20 pieces

## Ingredients:

- 1 cup blueberries
- 1/4 cup butter
- 3/4 cup coconut oil
- 1/4 cup cream cheese, softened
- 1/4 cup heavy cream
- 1 tsp stevia

## Directions:

1. Using a stand mixer, cream the butter and cream cheese together.
2. Add the stevia, heavy cream and coconut oil and mix until smooth.
3. Add the blueberries and mix until smooth.
4. Pour mixture into the wells of an ice cube tray and let sit in the freezer for an hour until firm.
5. Pop them out, serve and enjoy!

# 24. Blackberry Fat Bombs

**Time taken:** 20 minutes (plus 1 hour chilling)
**Servings:** 20 pieces

## Ingredients:

- 1 cup blackberries
- 1/4 cup butter
- 3/4 cup coconut oil
- 1/4 cup cream cheese, softened
- 1/4 cup heavy cream
- 1 tsp stevia

## Directions:

1. Using a stand mixer, cream the butter and cream cheese together.
2. Add the stevia, heavy cream and coconut oil and mix until smooth.
3. Add the blackberries and mix until smooth.
4. Pour mixture into the wells of an ice cube tray and let sit in the freezer for an hour until firm.
5. Pop them out, serve and enjoy!

# 25. Strawberry Cream Cheese Fat Bombs

**Time taken:** 20 minutes (plus 1 hour chilling)
**Servings:** 20 pieces

## Ingredients:

- 1 cup strawberries, chopped
- 1/4 cup butter
- 3/4 cup coconut oil
- 1/4 cup cream cheese, softened
- 1/4 cup heavy cream
- 1 tsp stevia

## Directions:

1. Using a stand mixer, cream the butter and cream cheese together.
2. Add the stevia, heavy cream and coconut oil and mix until smooth.
3. Add the strawberries and mix until smooth.
4. Pour mixture into the wells of an ice cube tray and let sit in the freezer for an hour until firm.
5. Pop them out, serve and enjoy!

# 26. Blueberry Crunch Cheesecake Fat Bombs

**Time taken:** 20 minutes
(plus 1 hour chilling time)
**Servings:** 12 balls

## Ingredients:

- 3/4 cup fresh blueberries, chopped
- 3/4 cup cream cheese, softened
- 1 tbsp heavy cream
- 1/4 cup butter, unsalted, softened
- 2 tbsp stevia
- 1 tbsp vanilla
- 1/4 cup corn flakes

## Directions:

1. Using a stand mixer, cream the butter and cream cheese together.
2. Add the stevia, heavy cream, and vanilla and mix until smooth.
3. Add the chopped blueberries and mix until smooth.
4. Cover the bowl with some cling wrap and let it sit in the fridge for 30 minutes until firm.
5. Remove the bowl from the fridge and roll mixture into small balls.
6. Roll the balls in the corn flakes to coat.
7. Add the balls to freezer for 30 minutes.
8. Serve and enjoy!

# 27. Mango Cheesecake Fat Bombs

**Time taken:** 20 minutes
(plus 1 hour chilling time)
**Servings:** 12 balls

## Ingredients:

- 3/4 cup fresh mango, chopped
- 3/4 cup cream cheese, softened
- 1 tbsp heavy cream
- 1 tbsp mango puree
- 1/4 cup butter, unsalted, softened
- 2 tbsp stevia
- 1 tbsp vanilla
- 1/4 cup crushed graham crackers

## Directions:

1. Using a stand mixer, cream the butter and cream cheese together.
2. Add the stevia, heavy cream, mango puree and vanilla and mix until smooth.
3. Add the chopped mango and mix until smooth.
4. Cover the bowl with some cling wrap and let it sit in the fridge for 30 minutes until firm.
5. Remove the bowl from the fridge and roll mixture into small balls.
6. Roll the balls in the crushed graham crackers.
7. Add balls to freezer for 30 minutes.
8. Serve and enjoy!

# 28. Apple Cinnamon Fat Bombs

**Time taken:** 30 minutes
(plus 1 hour 35 minutes chilling time)
**Servings:** 10 balls

## Ingredients:

- 1/3 cup chocolate protein powder
- 2 tbsp coconut flour
- 2 tbsp desiccated coconut
- 4 tbsp coconut milk
- 1 tbsp cocoa powder
- 1 Granny Smith apple, sliced
- 1 tsp cinnamon
- 1 tbsp sugar
- 1 tablespoon chocolate chips
- 3/4 cup white chocolate chips

## Directions:

1. In a large bowl, mix the protein powder, coconut flour, desiccated coconut and cocoa powder.
2. Add the milk and mix well.
3. In a small saucepan, cook the apple slices with the cinnamon and sugar.
4. Combine both mixtures in one bowl.
5. Cover the bowl with some cling wrap and let it sit in the fridge for 25 minutes until firm.
6. Remove the bowl from the fridge and roll mixture into small balls.
7. Line a baking sheet with parchment paper.
8. Place the balls on the baking sheet and freeze for 10 minutes.
9. Melt the white chocolate.
10. Remove the balls from the freezer and dip in white chocolate to coat.
11. Place the balls in the fridge to set, approx 1 hour.
12. Serve and enjoy!

# 29. Spiced Chocolate-Crunch Fat Bombs

**Time taken:** 20 minutes (2 hours chilling)
**Servings:** 10 squares

## Ingredients:

- 1 cup heavy cream
- 2 tbsp cocoa powder
- 1 tsp vanilla
- 1 tsp cinnamon
- 1/4 tsp cayenne pepper
- 2 tbsp stevia
- 3 tbsp corn flakes

## Directions:

1. Heat the heavy cream in a saucepan.
2. Add the cocoa powder, vanilla, cayenne pepper, stevia and cinnamon and whisk until smooth.
3. Pour the mixture into an ice-cube tray.
4. Top with corn flakes.
5. Freeze for about 2 hours.
6. Pop them out and serve. Enjoy!

# 30. Bacon and Cheese Bombs

**Time taken:** 40 minutes
(plus 30 minutes chilling time)
**Servings:** 6

## Ingredients:

- 2 large organic eggs
- 1/4 cup butter, salted
- 2 tbsp organic mayonnaise
- 1/4 tsp freshly ground pepper
- 1/4 tsp salt, to taste
- 6 small cubes sharp cheddar cheese
- 5 slices bacon

## Directions:

1. Preheat the oven to 190C/375F.
2. Line a baking pan with wax paper and lay the strips of bacon on it.
3. Let it cook in the oven for 12-15 minutes, until crisp.
4. While the bacon is in the oven, using a small pot, boil the eggs.
5. Add a pinch of salt to the water and let boil for about 12 minutes.
6. When the bacon is done, take it out of the oven, let it cool for a couple of minutes and chop into tiny bits.
7. Once the eggs are cooked, remove the hot water and replace it with cool water. Let eggs cool down and peel the shells off.
8. In a small bowl, mash the eggs with a fork.
9. Add the butter and mash together.
10. Add the mayo, mash together and season with a little bit of salt and pepper.
11. Cover the bowl with some cling wrap and let it sit in the fridge for 30 minutes, or until it firms up.
12. Remove the bowl from the fridge and roll the mixture into small balls.
13. Stuff each ball with a cube of cheddar cheese.
14. Roll the balls in the chopped bacon to coat.
15. Serve and enjoy!

# 31. Mocha Fat Bombs

**Time taken:** 20 minutes
(plus 1 hour chilling time)
**Servings:** 20 pieces

## Ingredients:

- 1 cup cream cheese
- 1/4 cup butter, unsalted
- 2 tbsp coconut oil
- 2 tbsp cocoa powder
- 1/4 cup stevia powder
- 10-15 drops stevia extract
- 1/2 cup strong brewed coffee
- 1 cup whipping cream

## Directions:

1. Using a food processor, mix the cream cheese, butter, coconut oil and cocoa powder.
2. Add the stevia powder and stevia extract and pulse until smooth.
3. Add the coffee, mix again and set aside.
4. Whip the cream until stiff peaks form.
5. Fold the whipped cream into the coffee mixture.
6. Pour the mixture into silicon molds and freeze for an hour or until it hardens.
7. Remove from the silicon molds and serve. Enjoy!

# 32. Strawberries & Cream Fat Bombs

**Time taken:** 20 minutes (plus 1 hour chilling time)
**Servings:** 20 pieces

## Ingredients:

- 1 cup cream cheese
- 1/4 cup butter, unsalted
- 2 tbsp coconut oil
- 1 tbsp strawberry extract
- 1/4 cup stevia powder
- 10-15 drops stevia extract
- 1/2 cup strawberry puree
- 1 cup whipping cream

## Directions:

1. Using a food processor, mix the cream cheese, butter, coconut oil and strawberry extract.
2. Add the stevia powder and stevia extract pulse until smooth.
3. Add the strawberry puree, mix again and set aside.
4. Whip the cream until stiff peaks form.
5. Fold the whipped cream into the the strawberry mixture.
6. Pour the mixture into silicon molds and freeze for an hour or until it hardens.
7. Remove from the silicon molds and serve. Enjoy!

# 33. Raspberry Mint Fat Bombs

**Time taken:** 20 minutes (plus 1 hour chilling time)
**Servings:** 20 pieces

## Ingredients:

- 1 cup cream cheese
- 1/4 cup butter, unsalted
- 2 tbsp coconut oil
- 1/4 cup stevia powder
- 10-15 drops stevia extract
- 3/4 cup raspberry puree
- 1 tsp peppermint oil
- 1 cup whipping cream

## Directions:

1. Using a food processor, mix the cream cheese, butter, coconut oil and peppermint oil.
2. Add the stevia powder and stevia extract and pulse until smooth.
3. Add the raspberry puree, mix again and set aside.
4. Whip the cream until stiff peaks form.
5. Fold the whipped cream into the raspberry mixture.

6. Pour the mixture into silicon molds and freeze for an hour or until it hardens.

7. Remove from the silicon molds and serve. Enjoy!

# 34. Herbed Cheese Fat Bombs

**Time taken:** 15 minutes
(plus 25 minutes chilling time)
**Servings:** 5 fat bombs

## Ingredients:

- 1/2 cup cream cheese
- 1/4 cup butter, salted, softened, cut into small pieces
- 1 tbsp fresh basil, chopped
- 1 tbsp fresh cilantro, chopped
- 5 olives, pitted and sliced
- 2 cloves garlic, crushed
- 1 tsp pepper
- 1/4 tsp salt, to taste
- 5 tbsp grated parmesan cheese

## Directions:

1. In a bowl, mash butter and cream cheese together with a fork.
2. Add the fresh basil, cilantro, olives and garlic.
3. Add salt and pepper, to taste.
4. Cover the bowl with some cling wrap and let it sit in the fridge for 25 minutes, or until it firms up.
5. Remove the bowl from the fridge and roll mixture into small balls.
6. Roll the balls in the parmesan cheese.
7. Serve and enjoy!

# 35. Spiced Nuts Fat Bombs

**Time taken:** 25 minutes
(plus 1 hour chilling time)
**Servings:** 8 mini squares

## Ingredients:

- 1/4 cup almond butter
- 1/3 cup heavy cream
- 2 tbsp coconut oil
- 1 tsp cocoa powder
- 1/2 tsp allspice
- 1/8 tsp nutmeg
- 8 drops stevia extract
- 1/4 cup macadamia nuts, crushed

## Directions:

1. Using a food processor, mix almond butter, heavy cream, coconut oil and cocoa powder and blend for about 2 minutes until smooth.
2. Add the stevia extract, nutmeg and allspice and blend again.
3. Pour mixture into a square 6x6 inch baking pan lined with parchment paper.
4. Sprinkle the top with the crushed macadamia nuts.
5. Place it in the fridge for about an hour until it hardens.
6. Remove from the pan and cut into small squares.
7. Serve and enjoy!

# 36. Vanilla Nut Fat Bombs

**Time taken:** 15 minutes
(plus 50 minutes chilling time)
**Servings:** 8

## Ingredients:

- 1/2 cup butter, unsalted, softened
- 4 tbsp heavy cream
- 2 tsp vanilla extract
- 8 tbsp coconut oil
- 3 tbsp cocoa powder
- 1 tbsp coffee (or espresso)
- 1 tsp stevia extract
- 1/2 cup dark chocolate, melted
- 1/4 cup crushed walnuts

## Directions:

1. In a bowl, mix the butter, cream and vanilla.
2. In a separate bowl, mix the coconut oil, cocoa powder, coffee (or espresso) and stevia extract.
3. Line 8 wells of a mini-muffin pan with wax paper liners.
4. Pour in the vanilla mixture and let harden in the freezer for about 20 minutes.
5. Remove the pan from the freezer and pour in the mocha mixture.
6. Place the pan back in the freezer for another 20 minutes.
7. Take the pan out and add a thin layer of the melted dark chocolate.
8. Sprinkle the walnuts on top and freeze for another 10 minutes.
9. Remove them from the pan, serve and enjoy!

# 37. Triple Mocha-Strawberry Fat Bombs

**Time taken:** 15 minutes
(plus 50 minutes chilling time)
**Servings:** 8

## Ingredients:

- 1/2 cup butter, unsalted, softened
- 4 tbsp heavy cream
- 2 tsp strawberry extract
- 1/4 cup frozen strawberries
- 8 tbsp coconut oil
- 3 tbsp cocoa powder
- 1 tbsp coffee (or espresso)
- 1 tsp stevia extract
- 1/2 cup dark chocolate, melted

## Directions:

1. In a bowl, mix the butter, cream and strawberry extract.
2. In a separate bowl, mix the coconut oil, cocoa powder, and coffee (or espresso) and stevia extract.
3. Line 8 wells of a mini-muffin pan with wax paper liners.
4. Pour in the vanilla mixture and let harden in the freezer for about 20 minutes.
5. Remove pan from freezer and add the mocha mixture.
6. Place the pan back in the freezer for another 20 minutes.
7. Take the pan out and add a thin layer of the melted dark chocolate.

8. Add some strawberries on top and freeze for another 10 minutes.

9. Remove them from the pan, serve and enjoy!

# 38. Berry-Nutty Square Bombs

**Time taken:** 25 minutes
(plus 40 minutes chilling time)
**Servings:** 12

## Ingredients:

- 1/4 cup macadamia nuts
- 1/2 cup cream cheese
- 1 cup blackberries
- 3 tbsp mascarpone cheese
- 1 cup coconut oil
- 1 cup coconut butter
- 1/2 tsp vanilla extract
- 1/2 tsp lemon juice
- 1 tsp stevia extract

## Directions:

1. Line a 6x6 baking pan with wax paper.
2. Preheat the oven to 190C/375F.
3. Crush the macadamia nuts, press into pan to create the crust and bake for 10-12 minutes.
4. Remove from the oven and cool.
5. Spread a layer of cream cheese over the crust.
6. In a bowl, mix the blackberries, mascarpone cheese, coconut oil, coconut butter, vanilla, lemon juice and stevia.
7. Pour the mixture into the pan and evenly spread it out.
8. Freeze for 40 minutes.
9. Remove from pan and cut into 12 equal square slices.
10. Serve and enjoy!

# 39. Pumpkin Patch Fat Bombs

**Time taken:** 15 minutes
(plus 45 minutes chilling time)
**Servings:** 12

## Ingredients:

- 4 tbsp butter, unsalted, softened
- 2 tbsp coconut oil
- 1/2 cup boiled pumpkin
- 1/2 tbsp fresh parsley, chopped
- 1 tsp ginger, minced finely
- 1/2 tsp nutmeg
- 1/2 tsp cinnamon
- 1 tsp stevia extract

## Directions:

1. Place the pumpkin, parsley, ginger, nutmeg, and cinnamon in the bowl of a food processor and pulse until smooth.
2. Add the coconut oil and butter and pulse again.
3. Add the stevia and pulse until everything is incorporated.
4. Place the mixture into a bowl, cover with cling wrap and let chill for 30 minutes until it hardens.
5. Remove mixture from the fridge, scoop into balls and place on a baking sheet.
6. Smooth balls if necessary and chill for 15 minutes.
7. Serve and enjoy!

# 40. Spiced Almond-Macadamia Fat Bombs

**Time taken:** 25 minutes
(plus 1-2 hours chilling time)
**Servings:** 12

## Ingredients:

- 1/2 cup cocoa butter, melted
- 1/4 cup pistachios, chopped
- 1/2 cup macadamia nuts, chopped
- 2 cups almond butter
- 1 cup coconut oil, firm
- 1 tsp coconut milk
- 1 tbsp vanilla
- 1/4 tsp almond extract
- 2 tsp allspice
- 1/4 tsp Himalayan salt
- 1 tsp stevia extract

## Directions:

1. Melt the cocoa butter in a small saucepan over low heat.
2. Using a stand mixer, cream the almond butter and add the coconut oil.
3. Slowly add the coconut milk and vanilla to the almond butter mixture.
4. Add the allspice, salt and stevia extract to the almond butter mixture.
5. Mix in well until it turns light in color.
6. Add the cocoa butter and mix for 3-4 minutes.
7. Pour the mixture into a greased and lined baking pan.
8. Top with the chopped pistachios and macadamia nuts.
9. Chill for 1-2 hours until firm.
10. Remove from pan and cut into equal square slices.
11. Serve and enjoy!

# 41. 5-Spice Fat Bombs

**Time taken:** 15 minutes
(plus 45 minutes chilling time)
**Servings:** 12

## Ingredients:

- 1 cup cream cheese
- 1/2 cup stevia
- 1 tsp ginger powder
- 1 tbsp cinnamon
- 1/2 tsp garlic powder
- 1/2 tsp nutmeg
- 1/2 tsp cayenne pepper
- 3/4 cup coconut oil
- 1/4 cup dark chocolate chips, melted

## Directions:

1. Place cream cheese, stevia, ginger powder, cinnamon, garlic powder, nutmeg and cayenne pepper in the bowl of a food processor and blend until smooth.
2. Slowly pour the coconut oil into the mixture while blending.
3. Place the mixture in a bowl, cover with cling wrap and let chill for 30 minutes until it hardens.
4. Remove from the fridge, scoop into balls and place on a baking sheet.
5. Smooth balls as necessary and chill again for 15 minutes.
6. Add a little dollop of melted chocolate on top of each ball and chill.
7. Serve and enjoy!

# 42. Salted Maple-Bacon Fat Bombs

**Time taken:** 15 minutes
(plus 45 minutes chilling time)
**Servings:** 12

## Ingredients:

- 1 cup cream cheese
- 1/2 cup butter, unsalted
- 4 tsp bacon fat
- 4 tbsp coconut oil
- 8 bacon slices, cooked to a crisp and chopped
- 1/4 cup organic maple syrup
- 1/4 tsp Himalayan salt

## Directions:

1. Place cream cheese, butter, bacon fat, maple syrup, salt and about half of the bacon pieces in the bowl of a food processor and blend until smooth.
2. Slowly pour in the coconut oil while blending.
3. Place the mixture in a bowl, cover with cling wrap and let chill for 30 minutes until it hardens.
4. Remove from the fridge, scoop into balls and place on a baking sheet.
5. Smooth balls if necessary and top with the rest of the bacon pieces.
6. Chill again for 15 minutes.
7. Serve and enjoy!

# 43. Spiced Peanut Butter Delights

**Time taken:** 15 minutes
(plus 30 minutes chilling time)
**Servings:** 12

## Ingredients:

- 4 tbsp coconut oil, melted
- 3 tsp stevia extract
- 4 tbsp cocoa powder
- 1 tsp vanilla
- 1/4 cup almonds, chopped
- 1/4 tsp cinnamon
- 1/4 tsp nutmeg
- 1/2 c peanut butter
- 1/4 tsp Himalayan salt

## Directions:

1. Place coconut oil, stevia extract, cocoa powder and vanilla in the bowl of a food processor and blend until smooth.
2. Pour mixture into a bowl and fold in the almonds.
3. Pour mixture into a 6x6x4 baking pan greased and lined with parchment paper.
4. Mix cinnamon, nutmeg and peanut butter until smooth and spread over chocolate mixture.
5. Sprinkle the top with Himalayan salt.
6. Freeze the mixture for about 30 minutes, until it hardens.
7. Remove from the pan and cut into small square pieces.
8. Serve and enjoy!

# 44. Triple-Layer Choco-Peanut Cups

**Time taken:** 15 minutes
(plus 45 minutes chilling time)
**Servings:** 12

## Ingredients:

- 1 cup coconut oil, melted
- 1/4 cup cocoa powder
- 1/4 cup peanut butter
- 3 tsp stevia extract
- 1 tsp vanilla
- 1/4 cup desiccated coconut

## Directions:

1. Divide melted coconut oil into three parts.
2. Add cocoa powder and 8 drops stevia extract to the first portion of coconut oil and stir until smooth.
3. Add peanut butter and 3 drops stevia extract to the second portion of coconut oil and stir until smooth.
4. Add vanilla and 4 drops stevia extract to the third portion of coconut oil and stir until smooth.
5. Line 12 wells of a mini-muffin baking pan with wax paper liners.
6. Pour chocolate mixture into prepared pan and freeze for 15 minutes.
7. Add peanut butter mixture over chocolate and freeze again for 15 minutes.
8. Add vanilla mixture over peanut butter mixture, top with desiccated coconut and freeze for another 15 minutes until hardened.
9. Serve and enjoy!

# 45. Pumpkin Walnut Cheesecake Bites

**Time taken:** 15 minutes
(plus 2 hours chilling time)
**Servings:** 12

## Ingredients:

- 1/2 cup butter, softened
- 1 cup cream cheese
- 1/2 cup pumpkin puree
- 1/4 cup walnuts, chopped
- 3 tbsp stevia extract
- 1 tsp vanilla
- 1 tsp cinnamon
- 1 tsp nutmeg
- 1/4 tsp salt

## Directions:

1. Place butter, cream cheese, pumpkin puree, stevia extract and vanilla in the bowl of a food processor and blend until smooth.
2. Add cinnamon, nutmeg and salt and blend for another 2 minutes.
3. Line a 6x6 baking pan with parchment paper and grease the paper.
4. Pour mixture into pan, sprinkle with chopped walnuts and chill for 2 hours.
5. Remove from pan and cut into bite-sized pieces.
6. Serve and enjoy!

# 46. Pistachio Chocolate and Coconut Bites

**Time taken:** 20 minutes
(plus 50 minutes chilling time)
**Servings:** 12

## Ingredients:

- 1 cup coconut oil, softened
- 3 tbsp stevia
- 1 tsp vanilla
- 1/2 tsp cinnamon
- 2 cup coconut shavings
- pinch of salt
- 1/2 cup cream cheese
- 2 tbsp cocoa powder
- 1/4 cup pistachios

## Directions:

1. Place coconut oil, stevia, vanilla and cinnamon in the bowl of a food processor and blend until smooth.
2. Pour mixture into a bowl, fold in the coconut shavings and add a dash of salt.
3. Grease a 6x6 baking pan with parchment paper and grease the paper.
4. Pour mixture into pan and freeze for 20 minutes until hardened.
5. Blend the cream cheese and cocoa powder and spread over mixture in pan.
6. Sprinkle pistachios on top and place in the freezer for 30 minutes until the mixture has settled and hardened.
7. Remove from the pan and cut into bite-sized pieces.
8. Serve and enjoy!

# 47. Chocolate Almond Domes

**Time taken:** 20 minutes
(plus 1 hour 15 minutes chilling time)
**Servings:** 6

## Ingredients:

- 1/2 cup almond butter, softened
- 2 tbsp coconut oil, melted
- 2 tbsp cocoa powder
- 1 tbsp coconut flour
- 3 tbsp stevia
- 1 tsp vanilla
- 1/2 cup dark chocolate, melted
- 1/4 cup coconut shavings

## Directions:

1. Place almond butter, coconut oil, cocoa powder, coconut flour, stevia, and vanilla in the bowl of a food processor and blend until smooth.
2. Place mixture in a bowl, cover with cling wrap and let chill in fridge for 30 minutes until hardened.
3. Remove from fridge, scoop into balls and place on a baking sheet.
4. Smooth balls if necessary and chill again for 15 minutes.
5. Remove balls from the fridge, dip in melted chocolate to coat and sprinkle with coconut shavings.
6. Chill for 30 minutes.
7. Serve and enjoy!

## 48. Lemon Mint Cheesecake Bites

**Time taken:** 20 minutes
(plus 45 minutes chilling time)
**Servings:** 6

### Ingredients:

- 1/2 cup cream cheese, softened
- 1/4 cup coconut oil, melted
- 4 tbsp butter, unsalted, softened
- 1 tbsp lemon juice
- 2 tsp stevia
- 1 tsp peppermint oil
- 1/2 tsp vanilla
- 1 tbsp lemon zest

### Directions:

1. Place cream cheese, coconut oil, butter, lemon juice, stevia, peppermint oil and vanilla in the bowl of a food processor and blend until smooth.
2. Place mixture into a bowl, cover with cling wrap and let chill for 30 minutes until it hardens.
3. Remove mixture from fridge, scoop into balls and place on a baking sheet.
4. Smooth balls as necessary, sprinkle with lemon zest and chill again for 15 minutes.
5. Serve and enjoy!

## 49. Blueberries and Cream Fat Bombs

**Time taken:** 25 minutes
(plus 30 minutes chilling time)
**Servings:** 6

### Ingredients:

- 1/2 cup cream cheese, softened
- 3/4 coconut oil, melted
- 1 cup butter, unsalted, softened
- 1/4 cup coconut cream
- 2 tsp stevia
- 1/2 tsp vanilla
- 1 cup fresh blueberries

### Directions:

1. Using a stand mixer, blend cream cheese, coconut oil, butter, stevia and vanilla until smooth.
2. Slowly add the coconut cream and mix until smooth.
3. Add blueberries and mix on high speed to break up the fruit.
4. Line a 6x6 baking pan with parchment paper and grease the paper.
5. Pour mixture into baking pan and freeze for 30 minutes until hardened.
6. Remove from pan and cut into bite-sized squares.
7. Serve and enjoy!

## 50. Strawberry Nuts and Cream Fat Bombs

**Time taken:** 25 minutes
(plus 30 minutes chilling time)
**Servings:** 6

### Ingredients:

- 1/2 cup cream cheese, softened
- 1 cup fresh strawberries
- 1 cup butter, unsalted, softened

- 1/4 cup coconut cream
- 3/4 coconut oil, melted
- 1/2 tsp vanilla
- 1/2 tsp strawberry extract
- 2 tsp stevia
- 1/4 cup walnuts, chopped

**Directions:**

1. Using a stand mixer, mix cream cheese, coconut oil, butter, stevia, strawberry extract and vanilla and blend until smooth.
2. Slowly add the coconut cream and mix until smooth.
3. Add the strawberries and mix them on high speed to break up the fruit.
4. Line a 6x6 baking pan with parchment paper and grease the paper.
5. Pour mixture into baking pan, sprinkle with the chopped walnuts and the pan to the freezer for 30 minutes until mixture becomes hardened.
6. Remove from the pan and slice into bite-sized squares.
7. Serve and enjoy!

# 51. Spiced Nutter Butter Fat Bombs

**Time taken:** 20 minutes
(plus 30 minutes chilling)
**Servings:** 6

## Ingredients:

- 1/2 cup butter, unsalted, softened
- 1/2 cup almond butter
- 1/2 coconut oil, melted
- 3 tsp stevia
- 1 tsp almond extract
- 1/4 tsp nutmeg
- 1/4 tsp allspice
- 1/4 cup walnuts, chopped
- 1/4 cup dark chocolate chips, melted

**Directions:**

1. Using a stand mixer, cream the butter, almond butter, coconut oil and stevia until smooth.
2. Add the almond extract, nutmeg and allspice and mix at high speed for 2 minutes.
3. Pour mixture into ice-cube tray.
4. Freeze for 30 minutes and pop them out.
5. Dollop a little melted chocolate on top and sprinkle with walnuts.
6. Place in small cupcake liners, serve and enjoy!

# 52. Homemade Spiced Buttermints

**Time taken:** 15 minutes
(plus 3 hours chilling time)
**Servings:** 15

## Ingredients:

- 1/2 cup butter, unsalted, softened
- 1/4 tsp peppermint oil

- 3 tbsp raw honey
- pinch of salt
- 1/8 tsp allspice

**Directions:**

1. Using a stand mixer, cream the butter, honey, salt, allspice and peppermint oil until light and fluffy.
2. Using a spatula, scrape mixture into a piping bag with a star tip.
3. Pipe mixture into mini-swirls onto a baking sheet lined with parchment paper.
4. Freeze for about 2 hours and move to the fridge for another hour.
5. When hardened, share and enjoy!

# 53. Homemade Cinnamon Buttermints

**Time taken:** 15 minutes
(plus 3 hours chilling time)
**Servings:** 15

## Ingredients:

- 1/2 cup butter, unsalted, softened
- 1/4 tsp peppermint oil
- 3 tbsp raw honey
- pinch salt
- 1/4 tsp cinnamon

**Directions:**

1. Using a stand mixer, cream the butter, honey, salt, cinnamon and peppermint oil until light and fluffy.
2. Using a spatula, scrape mixture into a piping bag with a star tip.
3. Pipe mixture into mini-swirls on a baking sheet lined with parchment paper.
4. Freeze for about 2 hours and move to the fridge for another hour.
5. When hardened, share and enjoy!

# 54. Peanut Butter and Chocolate Fat Bombs

**Time Taken:** 15 minutes
(plus 1 hour chilling time)
**Servings:** 4

## Ingredients:

- 4 tbsp peanut butter
- sea salt (as needed)
- 1 tsp vanilla extract
- 3 tsp truvia sweetener
- 4 tbsp dark chocolate cocoa
- 4 tbsp coconut oil

**Directions:**

1. Add the coconut oil to a microwaveable bowl and then place it in the microwave for 45 seconds to soften it up.
2. Add in the vanilla, truvia and cocoa and mix well.
3. Add the mixture into silicone cups, add in a dollop of peanut butter to each and top with sea salt.
4. Place in the freezing for at least 1 hour to harden up the fat bombs.

# 55. Ginger and Vanilla Fat Bombs

**Time Taken:** 10 minutes
(plus 1 hour chilling time)
**Servings:** 10

## Ingredients:

- 3 tbsp coconut oil, softened
- 2 tbsp coconut butter, softened
- 1/2 teaspoon powdered ginger
- 1 tsp stevia
- 1/2 vanilla bean

## Directions:

1. Combine all of the ingredients and mix until the stevia has dissolved completely.
2. Add the results to the molds of your choice and let them set in the fridge for at least 1 hour before serving.

# 56. Healthy Chocolate Mousse

**Time taken:** 15 minutes
(plus 30 minutes chilling time)
**Servings:** 2

## Ingredients:

- 1 cup coconut milk, refrigerated overnight
- 3 tbsp cocoa powder
- 1/2 tsp cinnamon
- 6-12 drops stevia extract
- 2 tbsp coconut flakes
- 2 tbsp unsweetened chocolate chips
- 1 tbsp almond flakes

## Directions:

1. Using a hand mixer, mix cocoa powder and coconut milk until smooth and no lumps remain.
2. Add cinnamon and stevia and whip until incorporated completely.
3. Transfer mixture to a piping bag and pipe into glasses or dessert bowls.
4. Sprinkle mousse with almonds, coconut flakes and chocolate chips.
5. Chill for 30 minutes.
6. Serve and enjoy!

# 57. Vanilla Mousse

**Time taken:** 15 minutes
(plus 30 minutes chilling time)
**Servings:** 2

## Ingredients:

- 1 cup coconut milk, chilled overnight
- 1 tbsp vanilla
- 1/2 tsp cinnamon
- 6-12 drops stevia extract
- 2 tbsp coconut flakes
- 2 tbsp white chocolate shavings

**Directions:**

1. Using a hand mixer, mix coconut cream and vanilla.
2. Add cinnamon and stevia and whip until incorporated completely.
3. Transfer mixture to a piping bag and pipe into glasses or dessert bowls.
4. Sprinkle mousse with coconut flakes and white chocolate shavings.
5. Chill for 30 minutes.
6. Serve and enjoy!

# 58. Strawberry Mousse

**Time taken:** 15 minutes
(plus 30 minutes chilling time)
**Servings:** 2

**Ingredients:**

- 1 cup coconut milk, chilled overnight
- 1/2 tbsp vanilla
- 1 tbsp strawberry extract
- 1/2 tbsp strawberry puree
- 6-12 drops stevia extract
- 1/4 cup fresh strawberries, chopped
- 2 tbsp white chocolate shavings

**Directions:**

1. Using a hand mixer, mix coconut milk, vanilla and strawberry extract.
2. Add the strawberry puree and stevia and whip until incorporated completely.
3. Transfer mixture to a piping bag and pipe into glasses or dessert bowls.
4. Sprinkle mousse with the fresh strawberries and white chocolate shavings.
5. Chill for 30 minutes.
6. Serve and enjoy!

# 59. Blueberry Mousse

**Time taken:** 15 minutes
(plus 30 minutes chilling time)
**Servings:** 2 servings

**Ingredients:**

- 1 cup coconut milk, chilled overnight
- 1/2 tbsp vanilla
- 2 tbsp blueberry puree
- 6-12 drops stevia extract
- 1/4 cup fresh blueberries, chopped
- 2 tbsp white chocolate shavings
- 2 tbsp walnuts, chopped

**Directions:**

1. Using a hand mixer, mix coconut milk and vanilla.
2. Add the blueberry puree and stevia and whip until incorporated completely.
3. Transfer mixture to a piping bag and pipe into glasses or dessert bowls.
4. Sprinkle mousse with the walnuts and white chocolate shavings.
5. Chill for 30 minutes.
6. Serve and enjoy!

# 60. Spicy Chocolate Mousse

**Time taken:** 15 minutes
(plus 30 minutes chilling time)

**Servings:** 2 servings

## Ingredients:

- 1 cup coconut milk, chilled overnight
- 3 tbsp cocoa powder
- 1/2 tsp cinnamon
- 1 tsp cayenne pepper
- 6-12 drops stevia extract
- 2 tbsp coconut flakes
- 2 tbsp white chocolate shavings
- 1 tbsp almond flakes

## Directions:

1. Using a hand mixer, mix coconut milk and cocoa powder until smooth and no lumps remain.
2. Add cinnamon, cayenne pepper and stevia and whip until incorporated completely.
3. Transfer mixture to a piping bag and pipe into glasses or dessert bowls.
4. Sprinkle mousse with the coconut flakes, white chocolate shavings and almond flakes.
5. Chill for 30 minutes.
6. Serve and enjoy!

# 61. Triple Chocolate Mousse

**Time taken:** 15 minutes
(plus 30 minutes chilling time)
**Servings:** 2 servings

## Ingredients:

- 1 cup coconut milk, chilled overnight
- 3 tbsp cocoa powder
- 1/2 tsp cinnamon
- 1 tsp cayenne pepper
- 6-12 drops stevia extract
- 1/4 cup chocolate chips, melted
- 2 tbsp white chocolate shavings
- 1 tbsp almond flakes

## Directions:

1. Using a hand mixer, mix coconut milk and cocoa powder until smooth and no lumps remain.
2. Add cinnamon, cayenne pepper and stevia and whip until incorporated completely.
3. Transfer mixture to a piping bag and pipe it into glasses or dessert bowls.
4. Drizzle mousse with the melted chocolate and sprinkle with the white chocolate shavings and almond flakes.
5. Chill for 30 minutes.
6. Serve and enjoy!

# 62. Toffee-Pecan Fat Bombs

**Time taken:** 20 minutes
(plus 30 minutes chilling time)
**Servings:** 24 mini cups

## Ingredients:

- 1 cup coconut oil
- 2 tbsp butter, unsalted, softened
- 1/4 cup cream cheese
- 2/4 tbsp cocoa powder
- 1/2 cup peanut butter
- 2 tbsp toffee syrup
- 24 pecan halves

## Directions:

1. Mix butter and coconut oil in a double boiler over medium heat.
2. Remove from heat and set aside.
3. Using a mixer, cream the cream cheese, peanut butter and cocoa powder until smooth.
4. Slowly pour in the butter mixture.
5. Add toffee syrup and mix well until all ingredients are incorporated properly.
6. Pour mixture into wells of a non-stick mini muffin pan.
7. Add a pecan to each mini cup.
8. Freeze for 30 minutes until hardened.
9. Serve and enjoy!

# 63. Watermelon Mint Fat Bombs

**Time taken:** 20 minutes
(plus 30 minutes chilling time)
**Servings:** 24 mini cups

## Ingredients:

- 1 cup coconut oil
- 1/4 cup butter, unsalted, softened
- 1/4 cup cream cheese
- 1 tsp peppermint oil
- 2 tbsp watermelon syrup
- 24 walnut halves
- 1/4 coconut shavings

## Directions:

1. Mix butter and coconut oil in a double boiler over medium heat.
2. Remove from heat and set aside.
3. Using a mixer, beat cream cheese until smooth.
4. Slowly pour in the butter mixture.
5. Add watermelon syrup and peppermint oil and mix well until all ingredients are incorporated properly.
6. Pour into a non-stick mini muffin pan.
7. Add a walnut half to each mini cup and sprinkle with coconut shavings.
8. Freeze for 30 minutes until hardened.
9. Serve and enjoy!

# 64. CocoWalnut Fat Bombs

**Time taken:** 15 minutes
(plus 30 minutes chilling time)
**Servings:** 36 mini bites

## Ingredients:

- 6 cups coconut flakes
- 1/2 cup butter, unsalted, softened
- 1/2 tsp Himalayan salt
- 1 tsp cinnamon
- 1 tsp almond extract
- 1/4 cup raw honey
- 1/4 cup walnuts, chopped

## Directions:

1. In a food processor, grind coconut flakes to a thick paste.
2. Add butter, salt, almond extract, cinnamon and honey and blend until smooth.
3. Line a 6x6 baking pan with parchment paper and grease the paper.
4. Pour mixture into pan and top with the crushed walnuts
5. Freeze for 30 minutes until hardened.
6. Cut into bite-sized squares.
7. Serve and enjoy

# 65. 2-Minute Fat Bombs!

**Time taken:** 5 minutes
**Servings:** 8

## Ingredients:

- 8 oz cold cream cheese
- 1 package Jell-O gelatin or pudding mix

**Directions:**

1. Make sure cream cheese is cold enough to easily cut into small pieces.
2. Cut cream cheese into 8 small bite-size pieces.
3. Roll cream cheese pieces in the gelatin or pudding mix.
4. Serve and enjoy!

# 66. Coco-Green Tea Fat Bombs

**Time taken:** 10 minutes
(plus 50 minutes chilling time)
**Servings:** 20

## Ingredients:

- 1 cup coconut oil
- 1 cup coconut butter
- 1/2 coconut milk
- 1/2 tsp green tea powder
- 1 tsp vanilla
- 3 drops stevia
- 1 cup desiccated coconut
- 1 tbsp green tea powder

**Directions:**

1. Using a stand mixer, cream the coconut butter and coconut oil.
2. Add coconut milk, green tea powder, vanilla and stevia and mix well.
3. Cover mixture with cling wrap and chill for 35 minutes until hardened.
4. Scoop mixture into balls and place on a baking sheet lined with parchment paper.
5. In a small bowl, mix the desiccated coconut and green tea powder.
6. Roll balls in coconut mixture to coat and chill for another 15 minutes.
7. Serve and enjoy!

# 67. Cilantro Smoked Salmon Fat Bombs

**Time taken:** 20 minutes
(plus 30-35 minutes chilling time)
**Servings:** 6

- 1/4 tsp cayenne pepper
- pinch of salt and pepper to taste

## Ingredients:

- 1/2 cup cream cheese, softened
- 1/3 cup butter, unsalted, softened
- 50g smoked salmon
- 1 tbsp fresh lemon juice
- 2 tbsp fresh cilantro, chopped

## Directions:

1. Using a food processor, blend cream cheese, butter and smoked salmon.
2. Add lemon juice, cilantro and cayenne pepper.
3. Season to taste with salt and pepper and blend until smooth.
4. Line a baking tray with parchment paper.
5. Transfer mixture into a piping bag and pipe dollops onto baking tray.
6. Chill for 30-35 minutes.
7. Serve and enjoy!

# 68. Pepper Mozzarella Sticks

**Time taken:** 20 minutes
**Servings:** 8

## Ingredients:

- 8 oz mozzarella cheese
- 8 thin slices bacon
- 1/4 cup coconut oil
- 1 tsp chili pepper
- 1 tbsp fresh parsley, chopped finely

## Directions:

1. Cut mozzarella into 8 equal sticks.
2. Mix chili pepper and parsley.
3. Roll mozzarella sticks in chili mixture to coat.
4. Wrap mozzarella sticks in bacon slices and fasten with toothpicks.
5. Heat coconut oil in a medium skillet over high heat.
6. Fry mozzarella sticks in oil for 3-5 minutes and drain on a wire rack.
7. Serve and enjoy!

# 69. Pizza Mozzarella Sticks Wrapped in Bacon

**Time Taken:** 15 minutes
**Servings:** 2

## Ingredients:

- pizza sauce (as much as desired)
- 1 cup, coconut oil
- 2 slices, bacon
- 1/2 cheese stick

## Directions:

1. Wrap each mozzarella stick half in bacon and secure it with the help of a toothpick.
2. Heat coconut oil in a medium skillet over high heat.
3. Fry mozzarella sticks in oil for 3-5 minutes and drain on a wire rack.
4. Fry the mozzarella stick halves for approx 3-5 minutes in .
5. Serve with pizza sauce (for the dip).

# 70. Deviled Eggs with Buffalo Chicken

**Time taken:** 30 minutes
**Servings:** 12

## Ingredients:

- black pepper (as much as desired)

- salt (as much as desired)
- 2 tbsp, blue cheese dressing
- 1 celery stick, finely chopped
- 1/4 cup buffalo wing sauce
- 1/4 cup blue cheese crumbles
- 1/4 cup onion, grated
- 6 oz. cooked chicken, chopped
- 6 organic eggs

## Directions:

1. In a large saucepan, add in the eggs before filling the pan with enough water that the eggs are submerged under 1 inch of water.
2. Add the pan to the stove over a saucepan turned to a high heat. After the water boils, remove the pan from the stove and let the contents cool for 12 minutes.
3. Peel the eggs and cut them in half vertically.
4. Add the yolks to a mixing bowl and mash well before adding in the remainder of the ingredients (except the chicken). Mash all ingredients together, except the chicken.
5. Add the chicken pieces to the egg halves and top with the yolk mixture.

# 71. Spicy Butternut Squash Fat Bombs

**Time taken:** 5-10 minutes
**Servings:** 12 servings

## Ingredients:

- 1 1/2 cup cream cheese, softened
- 4 tbsp sour cream
- 1/4 cup cooked and pureed butternut squash
- 1 tsp cayenne pepper
- 1 tbsp onion, minced
- salt and pepper to taste
- 8 slices bacon, cooked until crisp and chopped

## Directions:

1. In a large bowl, mash cream cheese with a fork.
2. Add sour cream, butternut squash, onion and cayenne pepper.
3. Add salt and pepper to taste and mix well.
4. Scoop mixture into balls and roll in the chopped bacon to coat.
5. Serve and enjoy!

# 72. Spicy Chorizo Fat Bombs

**Time taken:** 10 minutes
(plus 10 minutes chilling time)
**Servings:** 12 servings

## Ingredients:

- 1 1/2 cup cream cheese, softened
- 4 tbsp heavy cream

- 14 deli slices spanish chorizo, chopped
- 1 tsp paprika
- 1 tsp chili powder
- 1 tbsp fresh parsley, chopped
- 1 tbsp onion, minced
- salt and pepper to taste
- 8 slices bacon, cooked until crisp and chopped

**Directions:**

1. Pulse cream cheese, heavy cream, spanish chorizo, chili powder, onion, parsley and paprika in a food processor.
2. Add salt and pepper to taste and mix well.
3. Transfer mixture to a bowl and chill for 30 minutes.
4. Scoop mixture into balls and roll in the chopped bacon to coat.
5. Serve and enjoy!

## 73. Feta and Deviled Eggs

**Time taken:** 15 minutes
**Servings:** 12

### Ingredients:

- 6 large organic eggs, hard-boiled
- 1/4 cup onion, minced
- 1/4 tbsp garlic, minced
- 1/2 tbsp fresh parsley, chopped
- 1/4 cup feta cheese
- 2 tbsp fresh dill, coarsely chopped
- freshly ground pepper and salt, to taste

**Directions:**

1. Peel eggs and slice in half.
2. In a large bowl, mash egg yolks with a fork.
3. Add onions, garlic and parsley and mash together with a fork.
4. Add feta cheese and season with salt and pepper to taste.
5. Set egg halves cut-sides up on a baking tray lined with parchment paper.
6. Crumble yolk mixture into egg halves and sprinkle with dill.
7. Serve and enjoy!

## 74. Bacon & Cilantro Deviled Eggs

**Time taken:** 15 minutes
**Servings:** 12

- 1/2 tbsp fresh cilantro, chopped
- 2 tbsp fresh dill, coarsely chopped
- freshly ground pepper and salt, to taste

### Ingredients:

- 6 large organic eggs, hard-boiled
- 6 slices bacon, cooked until crisp and chopped
- 1/4 cup onion, minced
- 1/4 tbsp garlic, minced
- 1 tbsp olives, pitted and chopped

## Directions:

1. Peel eggs and slice in half.
2. Remove egg yolks.
3. Add bacon, onions, garlic, and cilantro to a bowl and mash together.
4. Add olives and season with salt and pepper to taste.
5. Set egg halves cut-sides up on a baking tray lined with parchment paper.
6. Top the bacon mixture into egg halves and sprinkle with dill.
7. Serve and enjoy!

# 75. Bacon with Capers Deviled Eggs

**Time taken:** 15 minutes
**Servings:** 12

## Ingredients:

- 6 large organic eggs, hard-boiled
- 6 slices bacon, cooked until crisp and chopped
- 1/4 cup onion, minced
- 1/4 tbsp garlic, minced
- 1/4 cup olives, pitted and chopped
- 2 tbsp capers, chopped
- 2 tbsp fresh dill, coarsely chopped
- freshly ground pepper and salt, to taste

## Directions:

1. Peel eggs and slice in half.
2. Add bacon, onions, garlic and capers to a bowl and mash together with a fork.
3. Add olives and season with salt and pepper to taste.
4. Set egg halves cut-sides up on a baking tray lined with parchment paper.
5. Top bacon and caper mixture into and over egg halves and sprinkle with dill.
6. Serve and enjoy!

# 76. Anchovy Deviled Eggs

**Time taken:** 40 minutes
**Servings:** 12

## Ingredients:

- 6 large organic eggs, hard-cooked
- 1/4 cup onion, minced
- 1/4 tbsp garlic, minced
- 1/4 cup olives, pitted and chopped
- 1 tbsp anchovies, chopped
- 1 tbsp capers, chopped
- 2 tbsp fresh dill, coarsely chopped
- freshly ground pepper and salt, to taste

## Directions:

1. Peel eggs and slice in half.
2. Add onions, garlic, and capers to a bowl and mash together with a fork.
3. Add olives and anchovies to the bowl and season with salt and pepper to taste.
4. Add mixture from the bowl into egg halves and sprinkle with dill.
5. Serve and enjoy!

# 77. Salami and Macadamia Fat Bombs

**Time taken:** 20 minutes
(plus 30 minutes chilling time)
**Servings:** 12

## Ingredients:

- 3 1/2 oz. Milano salami
- 1/4 cups macadamia nuts
- 3/4 cup cream cheese, softened
- 1 tsp Dijon mustard
- 6 slices bacon, cooked until crisp and chopped
- 1/4 tbsp garlic, minced
- freshly ground pepper and salt, to taste

## Directions:

1. In a food processor, mix salami and macadamia nuts until combined.
2. With a hand mixer, cream mustard and cream cheese until smooth.
3. Add garlic to cream cheese mixture, season to taste with salt and pepper and mix well.
4. Fold salami mixture into the cream cheese mixture and chill for 20 minutes.
5. Line a baking tray with parchment paper.
6. Scoop mixture into balls and roll in chopped bacon to coat.
7. Chill for another 10 minutes, serve and enjoy!

# 78. Bacon on Bacon Fat Bombs

**Time taken:** 15 minutes
(plus 30 minutes chilling time)
**Servings:** 12

## Ingredients:

- 3/4 cup cream cheese, softened
- 10 slices bacon, cooked until crisp and chopped
- 1/4 tbsp garlic, minced
- 1 tbsp coconut oil
- freshly ground pepper and salt, to taste

## Directions:

1. Divide chopped bacon into two portions.
2. Using a hand mixer, cream coconut oil and cream cheese until smooth.
3. Add one portion of the chopped bacon and mix well.
4. Chill for 20 minutes.
5. Line a baking tray with parchment paper.
6. Scoop mixture into balls and roll in remaining chopped bacon to coat.
7. Chill for another 10 minutes, serve and enjoy!

# 79. Cheddar and Ham Fat Bombs

**Time taken:** 15 minutes
(plus 30 minutes chilling time)
**Servings:** 12 servings

## Ingredients:

- 1 1/2 cup cream cheese, softened
- 4 tbsp heavy cream

- 1/2 cup grated cheddar cheese
- 14 slices deli ham, chopped
- 2 tsp olives, sliced
- 1 tbsp fresh parsley, chopped
- 1 tbsp onion, minced
- salt and pepper to taste
- 8 slices bacon, cooked until crisp and chopped

**Directions:**

1. Pulse cream cheese, heavy cream, ham and olives in a food processor.
2. Mix in onions, parsley and cheddar cheese.
3. Add salt and pepper to taste and mix well.
4. Transfer mixture to a bowl and chill for 30 minutes.
5. Scoop mixture into balls and roll in the chopped bacon to coat.
6. Serve and enjoy!

# 80. Fried Cauliflower, Bacon and Cheese Bites

**Time taken:** 30 minutes
(plus 2 hours 15 minutes chilling time)
**Servings:** 20

## Ingredients:

- 5 cups cooked cauliflower florets
- 10 strips bacon, cooked until crisp and chopped
- 1 cup cream cheese, softened
- 1/4 cup goat cheese
- 1 1/2 cup parmesan cheese, divided
- 1/2 cup cheddar cheese
- 3 cloves garlic, minced
- 1 tsp spanish paprika, divided
- 1 tsp garlic powder
- 1 cup breadcrumbs
- freshly ground pepper, to taste
- 1/2 cup coconut oil

**Directions:**

1. In a food processor, pulse cauliflower florets until texture resembles couscous.
2. In a large mixing bowl, thoroughly mix ground cauliflower florets, bacon, cream cheese, goat cheese, 3/4 cup parmesan cheese, cheddar cheese, garlic, Spanish paprika and garlic powder and season to taste with salt and pepper.
3. Chill mixture for 2 hours.
4. Mix remaining parmesan cheese and breadcrumbs.
5. Roll mixture into balls.
6. Roll balls in the parmesan cheese mixture to coat evenly and chill for 15 minutes.
7. Heat coconut oil in a deep large frying pan over high heat.
8. Fry the the balls in the coconut oil until golden brown.
9. Serve and enjoy!

# 81. Ham, Egg and Bacon Fat Bombs

**Time taken:** 15 minutes
(plus 5 minutes chilling time)

**Servings:** 12

## Ingredients:

- 3 large organic eggs, hard-boiled
- 1/4 cup butter
- 2 tbsp mayonnaise, organic
- freshly ground black pepper
- 1/4 tsp salt
- 5 slices cooked deli ham
- 5 slices bacon, cooked until crisp and chopped

## Directions:

1. Peel the hard-boiled eggs.
2. Chop ham into small squares.
3. In a bowl, mash eggs and ham together with a fork.
4. Add mayonnaise, season with salt and pepper to taste and mix well.
5. Cover the bowl with cling wrap and chill for 30 minutes until hardened.
6. Roll mixture into bite-size balls and chill for another 5 minutes.
7. Roll balls in chopped bacon to coat completely.
8. Serve and enjoy!

# 82. Zesty Fat Bombs

**Time taken:** 10 minutes
(plus 2 hours freezing time)
**Servings:** 16

## Ingredients:

- 4 tbsp butter, softened
- 4 tbsp coconut oil
- 1/4 cup cream cheese
- 4 tbsp heavy cream
- 2 tbsp lemon juice
- 1 tsp lemon extract
- 1 tsp stevia

## Directions:

1. Using a food processor, blend butter, coconut oil and cream cheese until smooth.
2. Add heavy cream, lemon juice and lemon extract and blend for 2 minutes.
3. Add stevia to taste and blend for another minute.
4. Pour mixture into an ice-cube tray and freeze for 2 hours until hardened.
5. Pop them out of the tray and serve.
6. Enjoy!

# 83. Strawberry Zest Fat Bombs

**Time taken:** 10 minutes
(plus 2 hours freezing time)
**Servings:** 16

## Ingredients:

- 4 tbsp butter, softened
- 4 tbsp coconut oil
- 1/4 cup cream cheese
- 4 tbsp heavy cream
- 2 tbsp strawberry puree
- 1 tsp lemon zest
- 1 tsp stevia

**Directions:**

1. Using a food processor, blend butter, coconut oil and cream cheese until smooth.
2. Add heavy cream, strawberry puree and lemon zest and blend for 2 minutes.
3. Add stevia to taste and blend for another minute.
4. Pour mixture into an ice-cube tray and freeze for 2 hours until hardened.
5. Pop them out of the tray and serve.
6. Enjoy!

# 84. Strawberry Almond Fat Bombs

**Time taken:** 15 minutes (2-3 hours chilling)
**Servings:** 16

## Ingredients:

- 4 tbsp butter, softened
- 4 tbsp coconut oil
- 1 cup strawberries, diced
- 3/4 cup heavy cream
- 2 tsp stevia
- 1 cup chocolate chips, melted
- 16 almonds

**Directions:**

1. Using a food processor, blend butter, coconut oil and strawberries until smooth.
2. Add heavy cream and stevia and blend for 2 minutes.
3. Pour mixture into an ice-cube tray to fill wells 3/4 full.
4. Freeze for 1 hour or until hardened.
5. Pour in the melted chocolate and top each bomb with one almond.
6. Freeze for 1-2 more hours.
7. Pop them out of the tray and serve.
8. Enjoy!

# 85. Blackberry Crisps Fat Bombs

**Time taken:** 15 minutes
(plus 1-2 hours chilling time)
**Servings:** 16

## Ingredients:

- 4 tbsp butter, softened
- 4 tbsp coconut oil
- 1 cup blackberries , diced
- 3/4 cup heavy cream
- 1/4 tsp peppermint oil
- 2 tsp stevia
- 1 cup chocolate chips, melted
- 1/4 cup rice crisps

**Directions:**

1. Using a food processor, blend butter, coconut oil and blackberries until smooth.
2. Add heavy cream and stevia and blend for 2 minutes.
3. Pour mixture into an ice-cube tray to fill wells 3/4 full.
4. Freeze for 1 hour or until hardened.
5. Pour in the melted chocolate and sprinkle with the rice crisps.
6. Freeze for 1-2 more hours.
7. Pop them out of the tray and serve.
8. Enjoy!

# 86. Cream Cheese Fluff Bombs

**Time taken:** 15 minutes
(plus 1-2 hours chilling time)
**Servings:** 24

## Ingredients:

- 1 cup cream cheese
- 1/2 cup butter, unsalted, softened
- 3/4 cup stevia
- 1/2 tsp vanilla

## Directions:

1. Using a stand mixer with whisk attachment, whisk cream cheese and butter on high speed until light in color.
2. Slowly add stevia and vanilla and whisk until light and fluffy (do not over-beat).
3. Transfer mixture to a piping bag.
4. Pipe mixture onto a baking tray lined with parchment paper into fluffy swirls.
5. Freeze for 1-2 hours and serve.
6. Enjoy!

# 87. Macadamia Cream Cheese Fluff Bombs

**Time taken:** 15 minutes
(plus 1-2 hours chilling time)
**Servings:** 24

## Ingredients:

- 1 cup cream cheese
- 1/2 cup butter, unsalted, softened
- 3/4 cup stevia
- 1/2 tsp vanilla
- 1/2 cup macadamia nuts, chopped

## Directions:

1. Using a stand mixer with whisk attachment, whisk cream cheese and butter on high speed until light in color.
2. Slowly add stevia and vanilla and whisk until light and fluffy (do not over-beat).
3. Transfer mixture to a piping bag.
4. Pipe mixture onto a baking tray lined with parchment paper into fluffy swirls and sprinkle with macadamia nuts.
5. Freeze for 1-2 hours and serve.
6. Enjoy!

# 88. Almond and Peanut Butter Fluff Bombs

**Time taken:** 15 minutes
(plus 1-2 hours chilling time)
**Servings:** 24

## Ingredients:

- 1 cup cream cheese
- 1/2 cup butter, unsalted, softened
- 2 tbsp peanut butter
- 3/4 cup stevia

- 1/2 tsp vanilla
- 1/2 cup almond flakes

**Directions:**

1. Using a stand mixer with a whisk attachment, whisk cream cheese, butter and peanut butter on high speed until light in color.
2. Slowly add stevia and vanilla and whisk until light and fluffy (do not over-beat).
3. Transfer mixture to a piping bag.
4. Pipe mixture onto a baking tray lined with parchment paper into fluffy swirls and sprinkle with almond flakes.
5. Freeze for 1-2 hours and serve. Enjoy!

# 89. Chocolate Spiced Fluff Bombs

**Time taken:** 15 minutes
(plus 1-2 hours chilling time)
**Servings:** 24

## Ingredients:

- 1 cup cream cheese
- 1/2 cup butter, unsalted, softened
- 1/4 tsp cinnamon
- 1/4 tsp nutmeg
- 1/4 tsp allspice
- 3/4 cup stevia
- 1/2 tsp vanilla
- 1/4 cup dark chocolate chips, melted

**Directions:**

1. Using a stand mixer with whisk attachment, whisk cream cheese and butter on high speed until light in color.
2. Slowly add cinnamon, nutmeg, allspice, stevia and vanilla and whisk until light and fluffy (do not over-beat).
3. Transfer mixture to a piping bag.
4. Pipe mixture onto a baking tray lined with parchment paper into fluffy swirls and drizzle with melted chocolate.
5. Freeze for 1-2 more hours and serve.
6. Enjoy!

# 90. Chocolate and Caramel Layered Bites

**Time taken:** 35 minutes
(plus 3 hours chilling time)
**Servings:** 24

## Ingredients:

- 3 cups milk chocolate chips
- 1 cup peanut butter
- 1/4 cup butter, unsalted, softened
- 1 cup caster sugar
- 1/4 cup evaporated milk
- 1 1/2 cup marshmallow fluff
- 1/4 cup peanut butter
- 1 cup pistachios, chopped
- 1/2 cup walnuts, chopped
- 1 tsp vanilla extract
- 2 cups caramel, melted
- 1/4 cup heavy cream

## Directions:

1. Line a 9x12 pan with parchment paper and grease the paper.
2. Melt milk chocolate chips and peanut butter in a double boiler and stir until smooth.
3. Divide mixture into two portions.
4. Pour one portion into the prepared pan, spread out evenly and freeze for 20 minutes.
5. Mix sugar and milk in a medium saucepan over medium heat and stir until the sugar is dissolved.
6. Add 1/4 cup peanut butter, vanilla and marshmallow fluff and stir well until smooth.
7. Add pistachios and walnuts and mix well.
8. Pour mixture into pan, spread evenly and freeze for 20 minutes.
9. Pour melted caramel into pan and freeze for 20 minutes.
10. Re-heat and stir remaining chocolate peanut butter mixture if necessary, spread evenly in pan and freeze for about 2 hours.
11. Remove from pan and cut into small square pieces.
12. Serve and enjoy!

---

# 91. Vanilla Berry and Caramel Layered Bites

**Time taken:** 35 minutes (plus 3 hours chilling time)
**Servings:** 24

## Ingredients:

- 3 cups white chocolate chips
- 1/4 cup heavy cream
- 1/4 cup butter, unsalted, softened
- 1 cup caster sugar
- 1/4 cup evaporated milk
- 1 1/2 cup marshmallow fluff
- 1/2 cup strawberries, chopped
- 1/2 cup blueberries, chopped
- 1/2 cup blackberries, chopped
- 1 tsp vanilla extract
- 2 cups caramel, melted
- 1/4 cup heavy cream

## Directions:

1. Line a 9x12 pan with parchment paper and grease the paper.
2. Melt white chocolate chips and peanut butter in a double boiler and stir until smooth.
3. Divide mixture into two portions.
4. Pour one portion into the prepared pan, spread out evenly and freeze for 20 minutes.
5. Mix sugar and milk in a medium saucepan over medium heat and stir until the sugar is dissolved.
6. Add 1/4 cup peanut butter, vanilla and marshmallow fluff and stir well until smooth.
7. Add strawberries, blueberries and blackberries and mix well.
8. Pour mixture into pan, spread evenly and freeze for 20 minutes.
9. Pour melted caramel into pan and freeze for 20 minutes.
10. Re-heat and stir remaining white chocolate and peanut butter mixture

if necessary, spread evenly in pan and freeze for about 2 hours.

11. Remove from pan and cut into small square pieces.
12. Serve and enjoy!

# 92. Coconut Chia Power Fat Bombs

**Time taken:** 25 minutes (plus 1 hour chilling time)
**Servings:** 10

## Ingredients:

- 3 tbsp chia seeds
- 1/2 cup coconut shavings
- 1/4 cup almond flakes
- 2 tbsp coconut flour
- 2 tbsp almond butter
- 1/4 heavy cream
- 1/4 cup stevia
- 1 tbsp coconut oil
- 1/4 cup maple syrup
- 1/4 tsp cinnamon
- 1/4 tsp nutmeg

## Directions:

1. In a double boiler over medium heat, combine stevia, coconut oil, maple syrup and almond butter.
2. Add cinnamon and nutmeg and stir well.
3. Transfer mixture to a bowl.
4. Add chia seeds, almond flakes, coconut shavings and coconut flour and mix well until everything is incorporated.
5. Line a 6x6 pan with parchment paper and grease the paper.
6. Pour mixture into pan and freeze for 1 hour until hardened.
7. Remove from the pan and cut into bite-size squares.
8. Serve and enjoy!

# 93. Vanilla Spice Candy Bombs

**Time taken:** 10 minutes (2 hours chilling)
**Servings:** 10

## Ingredients:

- 1 cup cream cheese, softened
- 1/2 cup stevia
- 1 tsp vanilla
- 1/2 cup heavy cream
- 1/4 tsp cinnamon
- 1/4 tsp nutmeg

## Directions:

1. Using a food processor, blend cream cheese and stevia.
2. Add vanilla and slowly add heavy cream.
3. Add cinnamon and nutmeg and blend until smooth.
4. Pour mixture into an ice-cube tray and freeze for 2 hours.
5. Pop candy out from the tray, serve and enjoy!

# 94. Chocolate Spiced Candy Bombs

**Time taken:** 10 minutes (2 hours chilling)
**Servings:** 10

## Ingredients:

- 1 cup cream cheese, softened
- 1/2 cup stevia
- 1t tsp vanilla
- 2 tbsp cocoa powder
- 1/2 cup heavy cream
- 1/4 tsp cinnamon
- 1/4 tsp nutmeg

## Directions:

1. Using a food processor, blend cream cheese and stevia.
2. Add vanilla and cocoa powder and slowly add heavy cream.
3. Add cinnamon and nutmeg and blend until smooth.
4. Pour mixture into an ice-cube tray and freeze for 2 hours.
5. Pop candy out from the tray, serve and enjoy!

# 95. Chocolate Raspberry Mint Candy Bombs

**Time taken:** 10 minutes (2 hours chilling)
**Servings:** 10

## Ingredients:

- 1 cup cream cheese, softened
- 1/2 cup stevia
- 1 tsp vanilla
- 1/2 tsp peppermint oil
- 1/2 tsp raspberry extract
- 2 tbsp cocoa powder
- 1/2 cup heavy cream
- 10 whole raspberries

## Directions:

1. Using a food processor, blend cream cheese and stevia.
2. Add vanilla, cocoa powder and raspberry extract, slowly add heavy cream and blend until smooth.
3. Place one raspberry in each well of an ice-cube tray.
4. Pour mixture over raspberries and freeze for 2 hours.
5. Pop candy out from the tray, serve and enjoy!

# 96. Coconut Berry Candy Bombs

**Time taken:** 10 minutes (2 hours chilling)
**Servings:** 10

## Ingredients:

- 1 cup cream cheese, softened
- 1/2 cup stevia
- 1 tsp vanilla
- 1/2 tsp coconut oil
- 2 tbsp cocoa powder
- 1/2 cup heavy cream
- 10 whole raspberries
- 1/4 cup coconut shavings

## Directions:

1. Using a food processor, blend cream cheese and stevia.
2. Add vanilla, coconut oil and cocoa powder, slowly add heavy cream and blend until smooth.
3. Place one raspberry and some coconut shavings in each well of an ice-cube tray.
4. Pour mixture into ice-cube tray and freeze for 2 hours.
5. Pop candy out from the tray, serve and enjoy!

# 97. Almond Macaroon Fat Bombs

**Time taken:** 25 minutes
(plus 30 minutes chilling time)
**Servings:** 10

## Ingredients:

- 1/4 cup almond flour
- 1/2 cup coconut shavings
- 2 tbsp stevia
- 1 tbsp vanilla extract
- 1 tbsp coconut oil
- 1/4 cup almond flakes
- 3 egg whites, chilled
- 1/4 cup dark chocolate chips, melted

## Directions:

1. Preheat oven to 200C/395F.
2. In a bowl, mix almond flour, coconut and stevia until well blended.
3. Melt coconut oil in a small saucepan and stir in the vanilla.
4. Remove from heat, pour into flour mixture and blend thoroughly.
5. Using a stand mixer and whisk attachment, whisk chilled egg whites until stiff peaks form.
6. Slowly fold egg whites into the flour mixture (do not over-mix).
7. Spoon mixture into wells of a greased non-stick greased mini muffin pan.
8. Bake for 8-12 minutes, remove from pan and let cool.
9. Drizzle bombs with melted chocolate and sprinkle with almond flakes.
10. Chill in the fridge for 30 minutes.
11. Serve and enjoy!

# 98. COCO-Nutty Fat Bombs

**Time taken:** 10 minutes
(plus 2 hours chilling time)
**Servings:** 10

## Ingredients:

- 1/2 cup coconut butter, softened
- 1/2 cup coconut oil, melted
- 1/4 cup desiccated coconut
- 1/4 cup walnuts, crushed
- 1/4 tsp vanilla
- 1 tsp stevia

## Directions:

1. Using a food processor, cream coconut butter and coconut oil.
2. Add vanilla and stevia and blend until smooth.
3. Add desiccated coconut and walnuts and blend for 20 seconds.
4. Pour mixture into wells of an ice-cube tray and freeze for 2 hours.
5. Serve and enjoy!

# 99. Ginger Coconut Fat Bomb

**Time taken:** 10 minutes
(plus 2 hours chilling time)
**Servings:** 10

## Ingredients:

- 1/2 cup coconut butter, softened
- 1/2 cup coconut oil, melted
- 1/4 cup desiccated coconut
- 1/2 tbsp ginger, crushed
- 1/4 tsp ginger powder
- 1/4 tsp vanilla
- 1 tsp stevia

## Directions:

1. Using a food processor, cream coconut butter and coconut oil.
2. Add vanilla and stevia, and blend until smooth.
3. Add the ginger and ginger powder and blend for 2 minutes.
4. Pour mixture into wells of an ice-cube tray and freeze for 2 hours.
5. Serve and enjoy!

# 100. Chocolate Coconut Truffle Bombs

**Time taken:** 10 minutes
(plus 2 hours chilling time)
**Servings:** 10

## Ingredients:

- 1/2 cup coconut butter, softened
- 1/2 cup coconut oil, melted
- 1/4 cup desiccated coconut
- 1/4 tsp peppermint oil
- 2 tsp cocoa powder
- 1 tsp stevia
- 1/4 cup unsweetened chocolate chips

## Directions:

1. Using a food processor, cream coconut butter and coconut oil.
2. Add vanilla and stevia and blend until smooth.
3. Add the cocoa powder and peppermint oil and blend for 2 minutes.
4. Sprinkle chocolate chips in wells of an ice-cube tray.
5. Pour mixture into ice-cube tray and freeze for 2 hours.
6. Serve and enjoy!

# 101. Goji Berry Fat Bombs

**Time taken:** 15 minutes
(plus 30 minutes chilling time)
**Servings:** 8-10

## Ingredients:

- 1 cup coconut oil, melted
- 1 tsp vanilla extract
- 1 tbsp stevia
- 1/2 tsp sea salt
- 4 tbsp cocoa powder
- 1/2 cup almond butter, softened
- 2 tbsp butter, unsalted, softened
- 1/4 cup walnuts, chopped
- 1/4 cup fresh goji berries

## Directions:

1. Using a food processor, blend coconut oil and vanilla extract.
2. Add stevia and salt.
3. Add the cocoa powder and blend until smooth and no lumps remain.
4. Add the almond butter and regular butter and blend for 3 minutes.
5. Line a mini cupcake pan with wax paper cup liners.
6. Fill cups 2/3 full and top with walnuts and goji berries.
7. Freeze for 30 minutes until firm.
8. Serve and enjoy!

# 102. Cocoa-Pistachio Fat Bombs

**Time taken:** 15 minutes
(plus 30 minutes chilling time)
**Servings:** 8-10

## Ingredients:

- 1 cup coconut oil, softened
- 1/4 cup coconut milk
- 1/4 cup almond butter
- 1/4 cup cocoa powder
- 15 drops liquid stevia
- 1 tsp vanilla extract
- 1/2 tsp almond extract
- 1/2 tsp Himalayan sea salt
- 1/4 cup pistachios, chopped

## Directions:

1. Using a food processor, blend coconut oil, almond butter and coconut milk.
2. Add stevia, vanilla extract and almond extract.
3. Add the cocoa powder and blend for 3 minutes until smooth and no lumps remain.
4. Line a mini cupcake pan with wax paper cup liners.
5. Fill cups 2/3 full and top with pistachios and salt.
6. Freeze for 30 minutes until firm.
7. Serve and enjoy!

# 103. Spiced Chocolate Walnut Cups

**Time taken:** 15 minutes
(plus 30 minutes chilling time)
**Servings:** 8-10

## Ingredients:

- 2 tbsp butter, softened
- 1 tbsp coconut cream
- 1 tbsp coconut oil
- 1 tsp cocoa powder
- 1/4 tsp cayenne pepper
- 1/4 tsp chili powder
- 1/4 tsp paprika
- 1 tsp stevia
- 1/4 cup walnuts, chopped

## Directions:

1. Using a food processor, blend coconut oil, butter and coconut cream.
2. Add stevia, cayenne pepper, chili powder and paprika.
3. Add the cocoa powder and blend for 3 minutes until smooth and no lumps remain.
4. Line a mini cupcake pan with wax paper cup liners.
5. Fill cups 2/3 full and top with chopped walnuts.
6. Freeze for 30 minutes until firm.
7. Serve and enjoy!

# 104. Mocha Latte Fat Bombs

**Time taken:** 15 minutes
(plus 1 hour chilling time)
**Servings:** 8-10

## Ingredients:

- 1/4 cup butter, softened
- 4 tbsp coconut cream
- 1/2 tsp vanilla
- 1/4 cup coconut oil

- 1 tbsp espresso powder
- 4 tsp stevia
- 1/4 tsp cinnamon

**Directions:**

1. Using a food processor, blend butter and coconut cream.
2. Add vanilla and cinnamon and blend for two minutes until smooth.
3. Line a mini cupcake pan with wax paper cup liners.
4. Pour in mixture to fill cups half full and freeze for 30 minutes.
5. Blend the coconut oil, espresso powder and stevia.
6. Mix well until everything is incorporated.
7. Pour espresso mixture over the vanilla mixture.
8. Freeze for another 30 minutes.
9. Serve and enjoy!

# 105. Cappuccino Fat Bombs

**Time taken:** 15 minutes (plus 30 minutes chilling time)
**Servings:** 8-10

## Ingredients:

- 1 cup coconut butter
- 1/3 cup coconut flakes
- 3 tbsp coconut oil
- 4 tbsp coconut cream
- 2 tbsp espresso powder
- 1 tsp vanilla
- 2 tsp stevia
- 1 tsp cinnamon

**Directions:**

1. Using a food processor, blend coconut butter, coconut cream, and coconut oil.
2. Add espresso powder, vanilla and stevia.
3. Add cinnamon and blend for 3 minutes.
4. Pour mixture into the wells of an ice cube tray and top with coconut flakes.
5. Freeze for 30 minutes until firm.
6. Serve and enjoy!

# 106. Ginger and Walnut Chocolate Bombs

**Time taken:** 15 minutes (plus 30 minutes chilling time)
**Servings:** 10-12

## Ingredients:

- 4 tbsp coconut oil
- 4 tbsp cocoa powder
- 2 tbsp coconut cream
- 12 walnut halves

- 1/2 cup butter, softened
- 2 tsp stevia
- 1 tsp vanilla extract
- 1/4 tsp ginger powder

## Directions:

1. Using a food processor, blend butter, coconut cream, and coconut oil.
2. Add vanilla and stevia.
3. Add cocoa powder and ginger powder and blend for 3 minutes.
4. Pour mixture into the wells of an ice cube tray.
5. Top each bomb with a walnut half.
6. Freeze for 30 minutes until firm.
7. Serve and enjoy!

# 107. Cookie Dough Fat Bombs

**Time taken:** 30 minutes
(plus 1 hour 35 minutes chilling time)
**Servings:** 14

## Ingredients:

- 2 cups almond flour
- 1/2 cup coconut oil
- 1 tsp vanilla
- 2 tsp stevia
- 1/4 tsp salt
- 1/2 cup dark chocolate chips
- 1 cup white chocolate chips, melted
- 1/4 cup colored sprinkles

## Directions:

1. Using a food processor, blend the almond flour, coconut oil, vanilla, salt and stevia.
2. Transfer to a large bowl and fold in the chocolate chips.
3. Knead dough and chill for 15 minutes.
4. Line a baking tray with parchment paper.
5. Roll out dough and cut into desired shapes with cookie cutters.
6. Chill cookies for another hour until hardened.
7. Dip cookies in white chocolate and decorate with colored sprinkles.
8. Chill for another 20 minutes and serve. Enjoy!

# 108. Ginger Spice Cookies

**Time taken:** 30 minutes
(plus 1 hour 15 minutes chilling time)
**Servings:** 14

## Ingredients:

- 2 cups almond flour
- 1/2 cup coconut oil
- 1 tsp vanilla
- 2 tsp stevia
- 1/4 tsp salt
- 1/4 tsp ginger
- 1/4 tsp cinnamon

**Directions:**

1. Using a food processor, blend the almond flour, coconut oil, vanilla, salt and stevia.
2. Transfer to a large bowl.
3. Add ginger and cinnamon.
4. Knead dough and chill for 15 minutes.
5. Line a baking tray with parchment paper.
6. Roll out dough and cut into desired shapes with cookie cutters.
7. Chill cookies for 2 hours or until hardened.
8. Serve and enjoy!

# 109. Allspice Chocolate Cookies

**Time taken:** 30 minutes
(plus 2 hours 35 minutes chilling time)
**Servings:** 14

## Ingredients:

- 2 cups almond flour
- 1/2 cup coconut oil
- 1 tsp vanilla
- 1/4 tsp salt
- 2 tsp stevia
- 2 tsp cocoa powder
- 1/4 tsp allspice
- 1/4 tsp nutmeg
- 1/4 tsp paprika
- 1/4 tsp cinnamon
- 1 cup white chocolate chips, melted

**Directions:**

1. Using a food processor, blend the almond flour, coconut oil, vanilla, salt and stevia.
2. Transfer to a large bowl.
3. Add allspice, nutmeg, paprika and cinnamon.
4. Knead dough and chill for 15 minutes.
5. Line a baking tray with parchment paper.
6. Roll out dough and cut into desired shapes with cookie cutters.
7. Chill cookies for 2 hours until hardened.
8. Dip cookies in the white chocolate.
9. Chill for another 20 minutes and serve. Enjoy!

# 110. Jalapeño Fat Bombs

**Time taken:** 20 minutes
(plus 40 minutes chilling time)
**Servings:** 10

## Ingredients:

- 1 cup cream cheese, softened
- 1/4 cup butter, softened
- 1/4 cup grated cheddar cheese
- 1 tbsp parsley, chopped
- 1/8 tsp pepper
- 2 jalapeño peppers, halved, seeded, and chopped finely
- 5 bacon slices, cooked until crisp and chopped

**Directions:**

1. Using a food processor, blend the cream cheese, butter and pepper.
2. Fold in the cheese, parsley and jalapeño peppers.
3. Refrigerate for 30 minutes until hardened.
4. Scoop mixture into balls and chill for 10 minutes.
5. Roll each ball in the chopped bacon to coat.
6. Serve and enjoy!

---

# 111. Bacon and Ham Fat Bombs

**Time taken:** 20 minutes
(plus 40 minutes chilling time)
**Servings:** 10

## Ingredients:

- 1 cup cream cheese, softened
- 1/4 cup butter, softened
- 1/4 cup grated cheddar cheese
- 1 tbsp cilantro, chopped
- 10 small cubes ham
- 1/8 tsp pepper
- 5 bacon slices, cooked until crisp and chopped

## Directions:

1. Using a food processor, blend the cream cheese, butter and pepper.
2. Fold in the cheddar cheese and cilantro.
3. Refrigerate for 30 minutes until hardened.
4. Scoop mixture into balls and press a cube of ham into each ball.
5. Chill for 10 minutes.
6. Roll each ball in the chopped bacon to coat.
7. Serve and enjoy!

---

# 112. Salami Bacon Fat Bombs

**Time taken:** 20 minutes
(plus 40 minutes chilling time)
**Servings:** 10

## Ingredients:

- 1 cup cream cheese, softened
- 1/4 cup butter, softened
- 1/4 cup grated cheddar cheese
- 1 tbsp basil, chopped
- 1/4 cup salami, chopped
- 1/8 tsp pepper
- 5 bacon slices, cooked until crisp and chopped

## Directions:

1. Using a food processor, blend the cream cheese, butter and pepper.
2. Fold in the basil, salami and cheddar cheese.
3. Refrigerate for 30 minutes until hardened.
4. Scoop mixture into balls.
5. Chill for 10 minutes.
6. Roll each ball in the chopped bacon to coat.
7. Serve and enjoy!

## 113. CocoLemon Fat Bombs

**Time taken:** 20 minutes
(plus 40 minutes chilling time)
**Servings:** 10

### Ingredients:

- 1 cup cream cheese, softened
- 1/4 cup butter, softened
- 1/4 cup coconut oil, softened
- 1 tsp stevia
- 1 tsp lemon extract
- 1 tsp vanilla
- 1/4 cup desiccated coconut

### Directions:

1. Using a food processor, blend the cream cheese, butter and coconut oil.
2. Add stevia, vanilla and lemon extract and mix well.
3. Refrigerate for 30 minutes until hardened.
4. Scoop mixture into balls.
5. Chill for 10 minutes.
6. Roll each ball in the desiccated coconut to coat.
7. Serve and enjoy!

## 114. Strawberry Coconut Fat Bombs

**Time taken:** 20 minutes
(plus 40 minutes chilling time)
**Servings:** 10

### Ingredients:

- 1 cup cream cheese, softened
- 1/4 cup butter, softened
- 1/4 cup coconut oil, softened
- 1 tsp stevia
- 1 tsp strawberry extract
- 1 tbsp strawberry puree
- 1 tsp vanilla
- 1/4 cup desiccated coconut

### Directions:

1. Using a food processor, blend the cream cheese, butter and coconut oil.
2. Add stevia, vanilla extract, strawberry extract and strawberry puree and mix well.
3. Refrigerate for 30 minutes until hardened.
4. Scoop mixture into balls.
5. Chill for 10 minutes.
6. Roll each ball in the desiccated coconut to coat.
7. Serve and enjoy!

## 115. Macadamia Pomegranate Fat Bombs

**Time taken:** 20 minutes
(plus 40 minutes chilling time)
**Servings:** 10

### Ingredients:

- 1 cup cream cheese, softened
- 1/4 cup butter, softened
- 1/4 cup coconut oil, softened
- 1 tsp stevia
- 3 tbsp pomegranate puree
- 1/4 cup macadamia nuts, crushed
- 1 tsp vanilla
- 1/4 cup desiccated coconut

## Directions:

1. Using a food processor, blend the cream cheese, butter and coconut oil.
2. Add stevia and vanilla.
3. Add the pomegranate puree and crushed macadamia nuts and mix well.
4. Refrigerate for 30 minutes until it hardened.
5. Scoop mixture into balls.
6. Chill for 10 minutes.
7. Roll each ball in the desiccated coconut to coat.
8. Serve and enjoy!

# 116. Banana Nut Fat Bombs

**Time taken:** 20 minutes
(plus 40 minutes chilling time)
**Servings:** 10

## Ingredients:

- 1 cup cream cheese, softened
- 1/4 cup butter, softened
- 1/4 coconut oil, softened
- 1 tsp stevia
- 1 banana
- 1 tsp lemon juice
- 1 tsp vanilla
- 1 tsp banana extract
- 1/4 cup desiccated coconut

## Directions:

1. Using a food processor, blend the cream cheese, butter and coconut oil.
2. Add stevia, banana extract and vanilla and mix well.
3. Mash banana and lemon juice together with a fork and blend into cream cheese mixture.
4. Refrigerate for 30 minutes until hardened.
5. Scoop mixture into balls.
6. Chill for 10 minutes.
7. Roll each ball in the desiccated coconut to coat.
8. Serve and enjoy!

# 117. Cucumber Mint Fat Bombs

**Time taken:** 20 minutes
(plus 40 minutes chilling time)
**Servings:** 10

## Ingredients:

- 1 cup cream cheese, softened
- 1/4 cup butter, softened
- 1/4 cup grated cheddar cheese
- 1 tbsp fresh mint, chopped
- 1/8 tsp pepper
- 1/4 cup cucumber, minced
- 5 bacon slices, cooked until crisp and chopped

## Directions:

1. Using a food processor, blend the cream cheese, butter and pepper.
2. Fold in the cucumber, cheese and mint.
3. Refrigerate for 30 minutes until hardened.
4. Scoop mixture into balls and chill for 10 minutes.
5. Roll each ball in the chopped bacon to coat.
6. Serve and enjoy!

## 118. Mexican Fat Bombs

**Time taken:** 20 minutes
(plus 40 minutes chilling time)
**Servings:** 10

### Ingredients:

- 1 cup cream cheese, softened
- 1/4 cup butter, softened
- 1/4 cup grated cheddar cheese
- 1 tbsp fresh mint, chopped
- 1 tbsp fresh coriander, chopped
- 1/8 tsp pepper
- 1/4 paprika
- 1/4 cup cucumber, minced
- 2 tbsp corn kernels
- 5 bacon slices, cooked until crisp and chopped

### Directions:

1. Using a food processor, blend the cream cheese, butter and pepper.
2. Fold in the cucumber, cheese and mint.
3. Add the coriander, paprika and corn kernels and mix well.
4. Refrigerate for 30 minutes until hardened.
5. Scoop mixture into balls and chill for 10 minutes.
6. Roll each ball in the chopped bacon to coat.
7. Serve and enjoy!

## 119. Hawaiian Fat Bombs

**Time taken:** 20 minutes
(plus 40 minutes chilling time)
**Servings:** 10

### Ingredients:

- 1 cup cream cheese, softened
- 1/4 cup butter, softened
- 1/4 cup grated cheddar cheese
- 1/8 tsp pepper
- 1/4 cup minced pineapple
- 1/4 cup chopped deli ham slices
- 5 bacon slices, cooked until crisp and chopped

### Directions:

1. Using a food processor, blend the cream cheese, butter and pepper.
2. Fold in the pineapple, cheese and ham.
3. Refrigerate for 30 minutes until hardened.
4. Scoop mixture into balls and chill for 10 minutes.
5. Roll each ball in the chopped bacon to coat.
6. Serve and enjoy!

## 120. Turkey Fat Bombs

**Time taken:** 20 minutes
(plus 40 minutes chilling time)
**Servings:** 10

### Ingredients:

- 1 cup cream cheese, softened
- 1/4 cup butter, softened
- 1/4 cup grated cheddar cheese

- 1/8 tsp pepper
- 1 tbsp minced onion
- 1/4 cup chopped deli turkey slices
- 5 bacon slices, cooked until crisp and chopped

## Directions:

1. Using a food processor, blend the cream cheese, butter and pepper.
2. Fold in the onion, cheese and turkey.
3. Refrigerate for 30 minutes until hardened.
4. Scoop mixture into balls and chill for 10 minutes.
5. Roll each ball in the chopped bacon to coat.
6. Serve and enjoy!

# 121. Herbed Fat Bombs

**Time taken:** 20 minutes
(plus 40 minutes chilling time)
**Servings:** 10

## Ingredients:

- 1 cup cream cheese, softened
- 1/4 cup butter, softened
- 1/4 cup grated cheddar cheese
- 1/8 tsp pepper
- 1 tbsp minced onion
- 1 tbsp fresh dill, chopped
- 1 tbsp fresh basil, chopped
- 1 tbsp fresh rosemary, chopped
- 5 bacon slices, cooked until crisp and chopped

## Directions:

1. Using a food processor, blend the cream cheese, butter and pepper.
2. Fold in the onion and cheese.
3. Add the dill, basil and rosemary and mix well.
4. Refrigerate for 30 minutes until hardened.
5. Scoop mixture into balls and chill for 10 minutes.
6. Roll each ball in the chopped bacon to coat.
7. Serve and enjoy!

# 122. Blue Cheese Fat Bombs

**Time taken:** 20 minutes
(plus 40 minutes chilling time)
**Servings:** 10

## Ingredients:

- 1 cup cream cheese, softened
- 1/4 cup butter, softened
- 1/4 cup grated cheddar cheese
- 1 tbsp blue cheese
- 1/8 tsp pepper
- 1 tbsp minced onion
- 1 tbsp fresh dill, chopped
- 1 tbsp fresh basil, chopped
- 1 tbsp fresh rosemary, chopped
- 5 bacon slices, cooked until crisp and chopped

## Directions:

1. Using a food processor, blend the cream cheese, butter and pepper.
2. Fold in the onion, blue cheese and cheddar cheese.
3. Add the dill, basil and rosemary and mix well.
4. Refrigerate for 30 minutes until hardened.
5. Scoop mixture into balls and chill for 10 minutes.
6. Roll each ball in the chopped bacon to coat.
7. Serve and enjoy!

---

# 123. Hazelnut Coffee Fat Bombs

**Time taken:** 20 minutes
(plus 40 minutes chilling time)
**Servings:** 10

## Ingredients:

- 1 cup cream cheese, softened
- 1/4 cup coconut oil, softened
- 2 tsp stevia
- 4 tbsp heavy cream
- 2 tbsp hazelnut syrup
- 1 tsp coffee liqueur
- 1/4 cup hazelnuts, chopped

## Directions:

1. Using a food processor, blend the cream cheese and coconut oil.
2. Add stevia, coffee liqueur and hazelnut syrup.
3. Add the heavy cream and blend for 2 minutes.
4. Place mixture into a large bowl and cover with cling wrap.
5. Refrigerate for 30 minutes until hardened.
6. Scoop mixture into balls and chill for 10 minutes.
7. Roll each ball in the chopped hazelnuts to coat.
8. Serve and enjoy!

---

# 124. Almond Cappuccino Fat Bombs

**Time taken:** 20 minutes
(plus 40 minutes chilling time)
**Servings:** 12

## Ingredients:

- 1/2 cup coconut oil, melted
- 1/4 cup almond butter, melted
- 1/4 cup heavy cream
- 1/4 cup cocoa powder
- 1 tsp coffee liqueur
- 2 tbsp stevia
- 12 walnut halves

## Directions:

1. Whisk together the almond butter and the coconut oil.
2. Whisk in the heavy cream and cocoa powder.
3. Add the coffee liqueur and stevia and whisk thoroughly.
4. Pour mixture into the wells of an ice cube tray.
5. Top each bomb with a walnut half.
6. Freeze for 2 hours.
7. Serve and enjoy!

# 125. Mango and Orange Creamsicle Fat Bombs

**Time taken:** 15 minutes
(plus 2 hours chilling time)
**Servings:** 10

## Ingredients:

- 1/2 cup coconut oil, melted
- 3/4 cup cream cheese
- 1/2 cup heavy cream
- 1 tsp orange extract
- 3 drops orange flavoring
- 2 tbsp stevia
- 1/4 cup fresh mango, diced
- 1 tbsp orange zest

## Directions:

1. Using a food processor, blend the cream cheese and coconut oil.
2. Add in the heavy cream, orange extract and orange flavoring.
3. Add stevia and orange zest and blend for 3 minutes.
4. Place some diced mango in the wells of an ice cube tray.
5. Pour in the orange mixture.
6. Freeze for 2 hours until hardened.
7. Pop them out, serve and enjoy!

# 126. Ginger Orange Creamsicle Fat Bombs

**Time taken:** 15 minutes
(plus 2 hours chilling time)
**Servings:** 10

## Ingredients:

- 1/2 cup coconut oil, melted
- 3/4 cup cream cheese
- 1/2 cup heavy cream
- 1 tsp orange extract
- 3 drops orange flavoring
- 2 tbsp stevia
- 1/2 tbsp ginger, minced
- 1 tbsp orange zest

## Directions:

1. Using a food processor, blend the cream cheese and coconut oil.
2. Add the heavy cream, orange extract and orange flavoring.
3. Add stevia, ginger and orange zest and blend for 3 minutes.
4. Pour mixture into the wells of an ice cube tray.
5. Freeze for 2 hours until hardened.
6. Pop them out, serve and enjoy!

# 127. Strawberry-Mint Creamsicle Fat Bombs

**Time taken:** 15 minutes
(plus 2 hours chilling time)
**Servings:** 10

## Ingredients:

- 1/2 cup coconut oil, melted
- 3/4 cup cream cheese
- 1/2 cup heavy cream
- 1 tsp strawberry extract
- 3 drops pink flavoring
- 2 tbsp stevia
- 1/4 tsp peppermint oil
- 1/4 cup fresh strawberries, diced

**Directions:**

1. Using a food processor, blend the cream cheese and coconut oil.
2. Add the heavy cream, strawberry extract and pink flavoring .
3. Add stevia and peppermint oil and blend for 3 minutes.
4. Place some diced strawberries in the wells of an ice cube tray.
5. Pour in the the strawberry mixture.
6. Freeze for 2 hours until hardened.
7. Pop them out, serve and enjoy!

# 128. Cappuccino Creamsicle Fat Bombs

**Time taken:** 15 minutes (plus 2 hours chilling time)
**Servings:** 10

## Ingredients:

- 1/2 cup coconut oil, melted
- 3/4 cup cream cheese
- 1/2 cup heavy cream
- 2 tsp coffee liqueur
- 2 tbsp stevia
- 1/4 cup chocolate chips

**Directions:**

1. Using a food processor, blend the cream cheese and coconut oil.
2. Add the heavy cream and coffee liqueur.
3. Add stevia and blend for 3 minutes.
4. Place some chocolate chips in the wells of an ice cube tray.
5. Pour in the the coffee mixture.
6. Freeze for 2 hours until hardened.
7. Pop them out, serve and enjoy!

# 129. Pomegranate Creamsicle Fat Bombs

**Time taken:** 15 minutes (plus 2 hours chilling time)
**Servings:** 10

## Ingredients:

- 1/2 cup coconut oil, melted
- 3/4 cup cream cheese
- 1/2 cup heavy cream
- 2 tbsp pomegranate puree
- 2 tbsp stevia

**Directions:**

1. Using a food processor, blend the cream cheese and coconut oil.
2. Add the heavy cream and pomegranate puree.
3. Add stevia and blend for 3 minutes.
4. Pour mixture into the wells of an ice cube tray.
5. Freeze for 2 hours until hardened.
6. Pop them out, serve and enjoy!

# 130. Cantaloupe Creamsicle Fat Bombs

**Time taken:** 15 minutes (plus 2 hours chilling time)
**Servings:** 10

## Ingredients:

- 1/2 cup coconut oil, melted
- 3/4 cup cream cheese
- 1/2 cup heavy cream

- 2 tbsp cantaloupe puree
- 2 tbsp stevia

**Directions:**

1. Using a food processor, blend the cream cheese and coconut oil.
2. Add the heavy cream and cantaloupe puree.
3. Add stevia and blend for 3 minutes.
4. Pour mixture into the wells of an ice cube tray.
5. Freeze for 2 hours until hardened.
6. Pop them out, serve and enjoy!

# 131. Strawberry Lemonade Creamsicle Fat Bombs

**Time taken:** 15 minutes
(plus 2 hours chilling time)
**Servings:** 10

## Ingredients:

- 1/2 cup coconut oil, melted
- 3/4 cup cream cheese
- 1/2 cup heavy cream
- 2 tbsp strawberry puree
- 1 tsp lemon extract
- 2 tbsp stevia

**Directions:**

1. Using a food processor, blend the cream cheese and coconut oil.
2. Add the heavy cream and strawberry puree.
3. Add stevia and lemon extract and blend for 3 minutes.
4. Pour the mixture into the wells of an ice cube tray.
5. Freeze for 2 hours until hardened.
6. Pop them out, serve and enjoy!

# 132. Spicy Chocolate Creamsicle Fat Bombs

**Time taken:** 15 minutes
(plus 2 hours chilling time)
**Servings:** 10

## Ingredients:

- 1/2 cup coconut oil, melted
- 3/4 cup cream cheese
- 1/2 cup heavy cream
- 2 tbsp cocoa powder
- 1 tsp chocolate syrup
- 1/4 tsp cayenne pepper
- 2 tbsp stevia

**Directions:**

1. Using a food processor, blend the cream cheese and coconut oil.
2. Add the heavy cream and cocoa powder.
3. Add stevia, cayenne pepper and chocolate syrup and blend for 3 minutes.
4. Pour the mixture into the wells of an ice cube tray.
5. Freeze for 2 hours until hardened.
6. Pop them out, serve and enjoy!

# 133. Cheese and Hazelnut Fat Bombs

**Time taken:** 15 minutes
(plus 40 minutes chilling time)
**Servings:** 10

## Ingredients:

- 1 cup cream cheese, softened
- 1/4 cup hazelnut butter, softened
- 1/4 cup grated cheddar cheese
- 1 tbsp parsley, chopped
- 1/8 tsp pepper
- 1/4 cup hazelnuts, chopped

## Directions:

1. Using a food processor, blend the cream cheese, hazelnut butter and pepper.
2. Fold in the cheese and parsley.
3. Refrigerate for 30 minutes until hardened.
4. Scoop mixture into balls and chill for 10 minutes.
5. Roll each ball in the chopped hazelnuts to coat.
6. Serve and enjoy!

# 134. Bacon Zucchini Fat Bombs

**Time taken:** 15 minutes
(plus 40 minutes chilling time)
**Servings:** 10

## Ingredients:

- 1 cup cream cheese, softened
- 1/4 cup butter, softened
- 1/4 cup grated cheddar cheese
- 1/8 tsp pepper
- 1/4 cup zucchini, finely chopped
- 5 bacon slices, cooked until crisp and chopped

## Directions:

1. Using a food processor, blend the cream cheese, butter and pepper.
2. Fold in the zucchini and cheese.
3. Refrigerate for 30 minutes until hardened.
4. Scoop mixture into balls and chill for 10 minutes.
5. Roll each ball in the chopped bacon to coat.
6. Serve and enjoy!

# 135. Bacon Avocado Fat Bombs

**Time taken:** 15 minutes
(plus 40 minutes chilling time)
**Servings:** 10

- 1/4 cup avocado cubes
- 5 bacon slices, cooked until crisp and chopped

## Ingredients:

- 1 cup cream cheese, softened
- 1/4 cup butter, softened
- 1/4 cup grated cheddar cheese
- 1/8 tsp pepper

## Directions:

1. Using a food processor, blend the cream cheese, butter and pepper.
2. Fold in the avocado and cheese.
3. Refrigerate for 30 minutes until hardened.
4. Scoop mixture into balls and chill for 10 minutes.
5. Roll each ball in the chopped bacon to coat.
6. Serve and enjoy!

# 136. Bacon Parmesan Fat Bombs

**Time taken:** 15 minutes
(plus 40 minutes chilling time)
**Servings:** 10

## Ingredients:

- 1 cup cream cheese, softened
- 1/4 cup butter, softened
- 1/4 cup grated cheddar cheese
- 1/8 tsp pepper
- 1 tbsp grated parmesan cheese
- 10 cubes cooked ham
- 5 bacon slices, cooked until crisp and chopped

## Directions:

1. Using a food processor, blend the cream cheese, butter and pepper.
2. Fold in the cheddar cheese.
3. Refrigerate for 30 minutes until hardened.
4. Scoop mixture into balls and stuff each ball with a cube of ham.
5. Chill for 10 minutes.
6. Roll each ball in the chopped bacon and parmesan cheese to coat.
7. Serve and enjoy!

# 137. Bacon and Pesto Fat Bombs

**Time taken:** 15 minutes
(plus 40 minutes chilling time)
**Servings:** 10

## Ingredients:

- 1 cup cream cheese, softened
- 1/4 cup butter, softened
- 1/4 cup grated cheddar cheese
- 1 tbsp pesto
- 1/8 tsp pepper
- 1 tbsp parmesan cheese
- 10 cubes cooked ham
- 5 bacon slices, cooked until crisp and chopped

## Directions:

1. Using a food processor, blend the cream cheese, butter and pepper.
2. Fold in the cheddar cheese and pesto.
3. Refrigerate for 30 minutes until hardened.
4. Scoop mixture into balls and stuff each ball with a cube of ham.
5. Chill for 10 minutes.
6. Roll each ball in the chopped bacon and parmesan cheese to coat.
7. Serve and enjoy!

# 138. Organic Coconut Fat Bombs

**Time taken:** 10 minutes
(plus 45 minutes chilling time)
**Servings:** 10

## Ingredients:

- 1/2 cup coconut butter, softened
- 1/3 cup coconut oil, softened
- 1/2 cup coconut shavings
- 1 tsp vanilla
- 1 tsp cinnamon

## Directions:

1. Using a food processor, blend the coconut butter and coconut oil.
2. Add the vanilla and cinnamon.
3. Add the coconut shavings and mix well.
4. Pour the mixture into 10 silicon molds and freeze for 45 minutes.
5. Remove bombs from the molds and serve. Enjoy!

# 139. Kefir Almond Bites

**Time taken:** 10 minutes
(plus 45 minutes chilling time)
**Servings:** 10

## Ingredients:

- 1 cup kefir cheese
- 1/2 cup butter, softened
- 1/2 cup coconut oil, melted
- 1 tsp lemon juice
- 1/2 cup almonds, crushed
- 1 tbsp honey

## Directions:

1. Using a food processor, blend the kefir cheese, butter and coconut oil.
2. Add in lemon juice and honey.
3. Add the crushed almonds and mix well.
4. Pour the mixture into 10 silicon molds and freeze for 45 minutes.
5. Remove bombs from the molds and serve. Enjoy!

# 140. Raspberry Jell-O bombs

**Time taken:** 15 minutes
(plus 1 hour chilling time)
**Servings:** 10

## Ingredients:

- 1 package sugar-free raspberry Jell-O
- 1 tbsp gelatin powder
- 1 tbsp raspberry puree
- 1/2 cup boiling water
- 1/2 cup cold heavy cream
- 1/2 cup walnuts, crushed

## Directions:

1. Mix Jell-O and gelatin powder into boiling water and stir until dissolved.
2. Slowly add the cream while stirring.
3. Stir in raspberry puree and walnuts.
4. Pour into candy molds and let set in the fridge for about an hour.
5. Pop them out, serve and enjoy!

# 141. Crunchy Peanut Butter Mousse

**Time taken:** 10 minutes
**Servings:** 2

## Ingredients:

- 1/2 cup heavy cream
- 1 tbsp peanut butter
- 1 tsp stevia
- 1 tsp vanilla
- 1/4 cup macadamia nuts, crushed

## Directions:

1. Using a stand mixer with a whisk attachment, whisk heavy cream until it begins to thicken.
2. Add the peanut butter, stevia and vanilla and mix well.
3. Spoon mixture into small ramekins.
4. Top each serving with some crushed macadamia nuts.
5. Serve and enjoy!

# 142. Strawberry Mousse

**Time taken:** 10 minutes
**Servings:** 2

## Ingredients:

- 1/2 cup heavy cream
- 1 tbsp peanut butter
- 1 tsp stevia
- 1 tsp vanilla
- 1 tsp strawberry extract
- 1 tbsp strawberry puree
- 1/4 cup almond flakes

## Directions:

1. Using a stand mixer and whisk attachment, whisk the heavy cream until it begins to thicken.
2. Add the peanut butter, strawberry extract, strawberry puree, stevia and vanilla and mix well.
3. Spoon mixture into small ramekins.
4. Top each serving with some almond flakes.
5. Serve and enjoy!

# 143. Bacon Spinach Fat Bombs

**Time taken:** 30 minutes
(plus 40 minutes chilling time)
**Servings:** 10

## Ingredients:

- 1 cup cream cheese, softened
- 1/4 cup butter, softened
- 1/4 cup grated cheddar cheese
- 1/8 tsp pepper
- 1/4 cup spinach
- 1 tbsp onions, diced
- 5 bacon slices

## Directions:

1. In a small non-stick pan, cook bacon until crisp.
2. Remove bacon from pan, chop and set aside.
3. In the bacon fat, cook onions and spinach until the spinach is soft.
4. Using a food processor, blend the cream cheese, butter and pepper.
5. Fold in the spinach mixture and cheese.

6. Refrigerate for 30 minutes until hardened.
7. Scoop mixture into balls and chill for 10 minutes.
8. Roll each ball in the chopped bacon to coat.
9. Serve and enjoy!

## 144. Bacon Cilantro Fat Bombs

**Time taken:** 30 minutes
(plus 40 minutes chilling time)
**Servings:** 10

### Ingredients:

- 1 cup cream cheese, softened
- 1/4 cup grated cheddar cheese
- 1/8 tsp pepper
- 2 hard-boiled eggs
- 1/2 tbsp cilantro, chopped
- 5 bacon slices, cooked until crisp and chopped

### Directions:

1. In a large bowl, mash together eggs, cream cheese and cheddar cheese with a fork.
2. Add pepper and cilantro and mix well.
3. Refrigerate for 30 minutes until hardened.
4. Scoop mixture into balls and chill for 10 minutes.
5. Roll each ball in the chopped bacon to coat.
6. Serve and enjoy!

## 145. Bacon, Egg and Ham Fat Bombs

**Time taken:** 30 minutes
(plus 40 minutes chilling time)
**Servings:** 10

### Ingredients:

- 1 cup cream cheese, softened
- 1/4 cup grated cheddar cheese
- 1/8 tsp pepper
- 2 hard-boiled eggs
- 1/4 cup chopped deli ham
- 5 bacon slices, cooked until crisp and chopped

### Directions:

1. In a large bowl, mash together eggs, cream cheese and cheddar cheese with a fork.
2. Add pepper and ham and mix well.
3. Refrigerate for 30 minutes until hardened.
4. Scoop mixture into balls and chill for 10 minutes.
5. Roll each ball in the chopped bacon to coat.
6. Serve and enjoy!

## 146. Fully Loaded Fat Bombs

**Time taken:** 30 minutes
(plus 40 minutes chilling time)
**Servings:** 10

### Ingredients:

- 1 cup cream cheese, softened
- 1/4 cup grated cheddar cheese
- 1/8 tsp pepper

- 2 hard-boiled eggs
- 1/4 cup chopped deli ham
- 1/4 cup chopped salami
- 5 bacon slices, cooked until crisp and chopped

**Directions:**

1. In a large bowl, mash together eggs, cream cheese and cheddar cheese with a fork.
2. Add pepper, ham and salami and mix well.
3. Refrigerate for 30 minutes until hardened.
4. Scoop mixture into balls and chill for 10 minutes.
5. Roll each ball in the chopped bacon to coat.
6. Serve and enjoy!

# 147. English Breakfast Tea Fat Bombs

**Time taken:** 20 minutes
(plus 3 hours steeping/chilling time)
**Servings:** 10

**Ingredients:**

- 1/2 cup coconut oil, melted
- 3/4 cup cream cheese, softened
- 1/2 cup heavy cream
- 2 tea bags English breakfast tea
- 1 tsp lemon extract
- 2 tbsp stevia

**Directions:**

1. In a saucepan, heat heavy cream. Place tea bags in cream, cover pan and let steep for 1 hour.
2. Squeeze tea bags and stir cream.
3. Using a food processor, blend the cream cheese and coconut oil.
4. Add the cream mixture, stevia and lemon extract and blend for 3 minutes.
5. Pour mixture into the wells of an ice cube tray and freeze for 2 hours until hardened.
6. Pop them out and serve! Enjoy!

# 148. Matcha Tea Creamsicle Fat Bombs

**Time taken:** 15 minutes
(plus 2 hours chilling time)
**Servings:** 10

**Ingredients:**

- 1/2 cup coconut oil, melted
- 3/4 cup cream cheese, softened
- 1/2 cup heavy cream
- 2 tsp green tea powder
- 2 tbsp stevia
- 1/4 cup macadamia nuts, chopped

**Directions:**

1. Using a food processor, blend the cream cheese and coconut oil.
2. Add the heavy cream.
3. Add stevia and matcha powder and blend for 3 minutes.
4. Pour mixture into the wells of an ice cube tray and freeze for 2 hours until hardened.
5. Pop them out and serve! Enjoy!

# 149. Peppertastic Fat Bombs

**Time taken:** 20 minutes
(plus 40 minutes chilling time)
**Servings:** 10

## Ingredients:

- 1 cup cream cheese, softened
- 1/4 cup grated cheddar cheese
- 1/8 tsp pepper
- 1/8 tsp cayenne pepper
- 2 hard-boiled eggs
- 1/2 tbsp yellow capsicum, minced
- 1/2 tbsp red capsicum, minced
- 5 bacon slices, cooked until crisp and chopped

## Directions:

1. In a large bowl, mash together eggs, cream cheese and cheddar cheese with a fork.
2. Add pepper, cayenne, red capsicum and yellow capsicum and mix well.
3. Refrigerate for 30 minutes until hardened.
4. Scoop mixture into balls and chill for 10 minutes.
5. Roll each ball in the chopped bacon to coat.
6. Serve and enjoy!

# 150. Allspice Egg Fat Bombs

**Time taken:** 20 minutes
(plus 40 minutes chilling time)
**Servings:** 10

## Ingredients:

- 1 cup cream cheese, softened
- 1/4 cup grated cheddar cheese
- 1/8 tsp pepper
- 1/8 tsp cayenne pepper
- 1/8 tsp allspice
- 2 hard-boiled eggs
- 5 bacon slices, cooked until crisp and chopped

## Directions:

1. In a large bowl, mash together eggs, cream cheese and cheddar cheese with a fork.
2. Add pepper, cayenne, and allspice and mix well.
3. Refrigerate for 30 minutes until hardened.
4. Scoop mixture into balls and chill for 10 minutes.
5. Roll each ball in the chopped bacon to coat.
6. Serve and enjoy!

# 151. Honey Crunch Fat Bombs

**Time taken:** 20 minutes
(plus 2 hours chilling time)
**Servings:** 10

## Ingredients:

- 1/2 cup coconut oil, melted
- 3/4 cup cream cheese
- 1/2 cup heavy cream
- 2 tbsp raw honey
- 2 tbsp stevia
- 1/4 cup cereal, crushed

**Directions:**

1. Using a food processor, blend the cream cheese and coconut oil.
2. Add the heavy cream.
3. Add stevia and honey and blend for 3 minutes.
4. Pour mixture into the wells of an ice cube tray.
5. Top bombs with crushed cereal.
6. Freeze for 2 hours until hardened.
7. Pop them out and serve! Enjoy!

# 152. Purple Yam Fat Bombs

**Time taken:** 20 minutes
(plus 2 hours chilling time)
**Servings:** 10

## Ingredients:

- 1/2 cup coconut oil, melted
- 3/4 cup cream cheese
- 1/2 cup heavy cream
- 2 tbsp purple yam powder
- 1 tbsp ube (purple yam) extract
- 2 drops purple food coloring
- 2 tbsp stevia
- 1/4 cup coconut shavings

## Directions:

1. Using a food processor, blend the cream cheese and coconut oil.
2. Add the heavy cream, purple yam powder, ube extract and purple food coloring.
3. Add stevia and blend for 3 minutes.
4. Pour mixture into the wells of an ice cube tray.
5. Top bombs with coconut shavings.
6. Freeze for 2 hours until hardened.
7. Pop them out and serve! Enjoy!

# 153. Churkey Meatballs

**Time taken:** 1 hour
**Servings:** 12

## Ingredients:

- 3 cups ground chicken
- 1/2 cup breadcrumbs
- 2 tbsp minced onion
- 1 tbsp coriander, chopped
- 1/2 cup turkey ham, chopped
- 1/8 tsp pepper
- 1/8 tsp salt
- 2 cloves garlic, minced
- 1 egg, beaten
- 3 tbsp olive oil
- 1 cup tomato sauce
- 1/4 cup basil
- 1/2 cup mozzarella cheese

## Directions:

1. Preheat oven to 200C/390F.
2. In a large bowl, mix the ground chicken, onion, coriander, turkey ham and garlic.
3. Add the breadcrumbs, egg, salt, pepper and olive oil and mix well.
4. Mix tomato sauce and basil and pour into a ceramic baking pan.
5. Roll the meat mixture into ping-pong size balls and place in the baking pan.
6. Sprinkle with mozzarella cheese.
7. Bake for 40 minutes and check if meat is cooked through.
8. If not, bake for another 15 minutes.
9. Serve and enjoy!

# 154. Chicken Beef Meatballs

**Time taken:** 1 hour
**Servings:** 12

## Ingredients:

- 2 cups ground chicken
- 1 cup ground beef
- 1/2 cup breadcrumbs
- 2 tbsp onion, minced
- 3 tbsp carrots, minced
- 1 tbsp coriander, chopped
- 1/8 tsp pepper
- 1/8 tsp salt
- 2 cloves garlic, minced
- 1 egg
- 3 tablespoons olive oil

## Directions:

1. Preheat oven to 200C/390F.
2. In a large bowl, mix ground chicken, ground beef, onion, carrots, coriander, and garlic.
3. Add breadcrumbs, egg, salt, pepper and olive oil and mix well.
4. Roll the meat mixture into balls the size of ping-pong balls and place in a ceramic baking pan.
5. Bake for 45 minutes and check if meat is cooked through.
6. If not, bake for another 15 minutes.
7. Serve and enjoy!

# 155. Chicken and Pesto Meatballs

**Time taken:** 1 hour
**Servings:** 12

## Ingredients:

- 3 cups ground chicken
- 1/2 cup breadcrumbs
- 2 tbsp onion, minced
- 1 tbsp coriander, chopped
- 1/8 tsp pepper
- 1/8 tsp salt
- 2 cloves garlic, minced
- 1 egg
- 3 tbsp olive oil
- 1 cup pesto sauce
- 1/4 cup basil
- 1/2 cup mozzarella

## Directions:

1. Preheat oven to 200C/390F.
2. In a large bowl, mix ground chicken, onion, coriander, and garlic.
3. Add breadcrumbs, egg, salt, pepper and olive oil and mix well.
4. Mix pesto sauce and basil and spread in a ceramic baking pan.
5. Roll the meat mixture into balls the size of ping-pong balls and place in the baking pan.
6. Sprinkle with mozzarella cheese.
7. Bake for 40 minutes and check if meat is cooked through.
8. If not, bake for another 15 minutes.
9. Serve and enjoy!

# 156. Spiced Beef Meatballs

**Time taken:** 1 hour
**Servings:** 12

## Ingredients:

- 3 cups ground beef
- 1/2 cup breadcrumbs
- 2 tbsp onion, minced
- 1 tbsp coriander, chopped
- 1/4 tsp paprika
- 1/8 tsp allspice
- 1/4 tsp cayenne powder
- 1/8 tsp pepper
- 1/8 tsp salt
- 2 cloves garlic, minced
- 1 egg
- 3 tbsp olive oil
- 1/4 cup sriracha sauce

## Directions:

1. Preheat oven to 200C/390F.
2. In a large bowl, mix ground beef, onion, coriander, and garlic.
3. Add breadcrumbs, egg, paprika, allspice, cayenne, salt, pepper and olive oil and mix well.
4. Roll the meat mixture into balls the size of ping-pong balls and place in a ceramic baking pan.
5. Drizzle sriracha sauce over the meatballs.
6. Bake for 45 minutes and check if meat is cooked through.
7. If not, bake for another 15 minutes.
8. Serve and enjoy!

# 157. Curried Chicken Meatballs

**Time taken:** 1 hour
**Servings:** 12

## Ingredients:

- 3 cups ground chicken
- 1/2 cup breadcrumbs
- 2 tbsp onion, minced
- 1 tbsp coriander, chopped
- 1 tsp curry powder
- 1/8 tsp pepper
- 1/8 tsp salt
- 2 cloves garlic, minced
- 1 egg
- 3 tbsp olive oil

## Directions:

1. Preheat oven to 200C/390F.
2. In a large bowl, mix ground chicken, onion, coriander, and garlic.
3. Add breadcrumbs, egg, curry powder, salt, pepper and olive oil and mix well.
4. Roll the meat into balls the size of ping-pong balls and place in a ceramic baking pan.
5. Bake for 45 minutes and check if meat is cooked through.
6. If not, bake for another 15 minutes.
7. Serve and enjoy!

# 158. Chicken Parmigiana Meatballs

**Time taken:** 1 hour
**Servings:** 12

## Ingredients:

- 3 cups ground chicken
- 1/2 cup breadcrumbs
- 2 tbsp onion, minced
- 1/8 tsp pepper
- 1/8 tsp salt
- 2 cloves garlic, minced
- 1 egg

- 3 tbsp olive oil
- 3 tbsp parmesan cheese
- 1 cup tomato sauce
- 1/4 cup basil
- 1/2 cup mozzarella

**Directions:**

1. Preheat oven to 200C/390F.
2. In a large bowl, mix ground chicken, onion, and garlic.
3. Add breadcrumbs, egg, parmesan cheese, salt, pepper and olive oil and mix well.
4. Mix tomato sauce and basil and spread in a ceramic baking pan.
5. Roll the meat mixture into balls the size of ping-pong balls and place in the baking pan.
6. Sprinkle with mozzarella cheese.
7. Bake meatballs for 40 minutes and check if meat is cooked through.
8. If not, bake for another 15 minutes.
9. Serve and enjoy!

# 159. Chicken and Mushroom Meatballs

**Time taken:** 1 hour
**Servings:** 12

## Ingredients:

- 3 cups ground chicken
- 1/2 cup mushrooms, chopped
- 1/2 cup breadcrumbs
- 2 tbsp onion, minced
- 1/8 tsp pepper
- 3 tbsp parmesan cheese
- 1/8 tsp salt
- 2 cloves garlic, minced
- 1 egg
- 3 tbsp olive oil

**Directions:**

1. Preheat oven to 200C/390F.
2. In a large bowl, mix ground chicken, mushrooms, onion, and garlic.
3. Add breadcrumbs, egg, parmesan cheese, salt, pepper and olive oil and mix well.
4. Roll the meat mixture into balls the size of ping-pong balls and place in a ceramic baking pan.
5. Bake meatballs for 40 minutes and check if meat is cooked through.
6. If not, bake for another 15 minutes.
7. Serve and enjoy!

# 160. Olive and Pesto Pizza Balls

**Time taken:** 15 minutes
(plus 30 minutes chill time)
**Servings:** 14

## Ingredients:

- 1 cup cream cheese
- 1/4 cup sliced salami
- 2 tbsp pitted olives
- 2 tbsp red bell pepper, chopped
- 2 tbsp pesto
- 2 tbsp fresh basil, chopped
- salt and pepper to taste
- 14 tomato slices (from small- to medium-size tomatoes)

## Directions:

1. In a large bowl, mix cream cheese, basil, bell peppers, pesto and olives.
2. Add salami and a pinch of salt and pepper.
3. Mix thoroughly, cover bowl with cling wrap and chill for 30 minutes.
4. Roll mixture into balls.
5. Place each ball onto a slice of tomato and skewer with a toothpick.
6. Serve and enjoy!

# 161. Beef Jalapeño Fat Bombs

**Time taken:** 40 minutes
**Servings:** 14

## Ingredients:

- 3 cups ground beef
- 1 cup cream cheese
- 8 slices bacon, cooked until crisp and chopped
- 1 cup grated cheddar cheese
- 2 tbsp onion, finely diced
- 3 cloves garlic, minced
- 1 tsp cayenne pepper
- 1 tsp chives, chopped
- 3/4 tsp coarse salt
- 1/4 tsp black pepper
- 3 tbsp olive oil

## Directions:

1. Heat olive oil and garlic in a large non-stick pan over medium-high heat.
2. Add onions, beef, cayenne pepper, chives, salt and pepper and cook until meat is no longer pink.
3. Transfer meat mixture to a large bowl and let cool.
4. Add cream cheese and cheddar cheese and mix well.
5. Form mixture into balls the size of ping-pong balls.
6. Roll balls in the chopped bacon to coat. Serve and enjoy!

# 162. Chicken and Bacon Fat Bombs

**Time taken:** 40 minutes
**Servings:** 14

## Ingredients:

- 3 cups ground chicken
- 1 cup cream cheese
- 8 slices bacon, cooked until crisp and chopped
- 1 cup grated cheddar cheese
- 2 tbsp onion, finely diced
- 3 cloves garlic, minced
- 1 tsp paprika
- 1 tsp chives, chopped
- 3/4 tsp coarse salt
- 1/4 tsp black pepper
- 3 tbsp olive oil

## Directions:

1. Heat olive oil and garlic in a large non-stick pan over medium-high heat.
2. Add onions, chicken, paprika, chives, salt and pepper and cook until meat is no longer pink.
3. Transfer meat mixture to a large bowl and let cool.
4. Add cream cheese and cheddar cheese and mix well.
5. Form mixture into balls the size of ping-pong balls.
6. Roll in chopped bacon to coat. Serve and enjoy!

# 163. Pimento and Cheese Fat Bombs

**Time taken:** 25 minutes (plus 30 minutes chill time)
**Servings:** 14

## Ingredients:

- 1 cup cream cheese
- 3/4 tsp coarse salt
- 1/4 tsp black pepper
- 1/2 tsp Dijon mustard
- 8 slices bacon, cooked until crisp and chopped
- 1 cup grated cheddar cheese
- 3 tbsp pimento, finely diced
- 3 cloves garlic, minced
- 1 tsp paprika
- 1 tsp cayenne pepper

## Directions:

1. In a large bowl, mix cream cheese, cheddar cheese, pimento and garlic.
2. Add paprika, cayenne pepper, salt, pepper and Dijon mustard and mix well.
3. Cover bowl with cling wrap and chill for 30 minutes.
4. Scoop mixture into balls and roll in the chopped bacon to coat.
5. Serve and enjoy!

# 164. Texan BBQ Fat Bombs

**Time taken:** 15 minutes (plus 30 minutes chill time)
**Servings:** 14 balls

## Ingredients:

- 1 cup cream cheese
- 8 slices bacon, cooked until crisp and chopped
- 1 cup grated cheddar cheese
- 3 cloves garlic, minced
- 2 tsp Texan BBQ powder
- 3/4 tsp coarse salt
- 1/4 tsp black pepper

## Directions:

1. In a large bowl, mix cream cheese, cheddar cheese, and garlic.
2. Add Texan BBQ powder, salt and pepper and mix well.
3. Cover bowl with cling wrap and chill for 30 minutes.
4. Scoop mixture into balls and roll in the chopped bacon to coat.
5. Serve and enjoy!

# 165. Blue Bacon Fat Bombs

**Time taken:** 15 minutes
(plus 30 minutes chill time)
**Servings:** 14 balls

## Ingredients:

- 1 cup cream cheese
- 8 slices bacon, cooked until crisp and chopped
- 3/4 cup grated cheddar cheese
- 1/4 cup blue cheese
- 1/4 cup parsley, chopped
- 3 cloves garlic, minced
- 3/4 tsp coarse salt
- 1/4 tsp black pepper

## Directions:

1. In a large bowl, mix cream cheese, cheddar cheese, and garlic.
2. Add blue cheese, parsley, salt and pepper and mix well.
3. Cover bowl with cling wrap and chill for 30 minutes.
4. Scoop mixture into balls and roll in the chopped bacon to coat.
5. Serve and enjoy!

# 166. Turkey Bacon Fat Bombs

**Time taken:** 15 minutes
(plus 30 minutes chill time)
**Servings:** 12 servings

## Ingredients:

- 1 1/2 cup cream cheese, softened
- 4 tbsp heavy cream
- 14 deli slices turkey, chopped
- 1 tsp paprika
- 1 tbsp fresh parsley, chopped
- 1 tbsp onion, minced
- salt and pepper to taste
- 8 slices bacon, cooked until crisp and chopped

## Directions:

1. Pulse cream cheese, heavy cream, turkey, onion, parsley and paprika in a food processor.
2. Add salt and pepper to taste and mix well.
3. Transfer mixture to a bowl and chill for 30 minutes.
4. Scoop mixture into balls and roll in the chopped bacon to coat.
5. Serve and enjoy.

# 167. Zucchini and Bacon Fat Bombs

**Time taken:** 30 minutes
**Servings:** 12

## Ingredients:

- 1 large zucchini, minced
- 8 slices bacon, chopped
- 1 small white onion, minced
- 1 cup cream cheese
- 2 garlic cloves, minced
- 1 tbsp coconut oil
- 1 tbsp fresh chives, chopped

- 1 tbsp fresh cilantro, chopped
- salt and pepper to taste

**Directions:**

1. Cook bacon in a non-stick pan for 6 minutes until crisp.
2. Add coconut oil, garlic and onion.
3. Add zucchini, chives and cilantro.
4. Add a dash of salt and pepper to taste.
5. Cook for another 3-5 minutes until zucchini is tender.
6. Transfer mixture to a bowl and let cool.
7. Add cream cheese and mix well.
8. Scoop mixture into balls and serve. Enjoy!

# 168. Cucumber Bacon Fat Bombs

**Time taken:** 30 minutes
**Servings:** 12

## Ingredients:

- 8 slices bacon, chopped
- 1 large cucumber, minced
- 1 small white onion, minced
- 1 cup cream cheese
- 2 garlic cloves, minced
- 1 tbsp coconut oil
- 1 tbsp fresh chives, chopped
- salt and pepper to taste

**Directions:**

1. Cook bacon in a non-stick pan for 6 minutes until crisp.
2. Add coconut oil, garlic and onion.
3. Add cucumber and chives.
4. Add a dash of salt and pepper to taste.
5. Cook for another 3-5 minutes until cucumber is tender.
6. Transfer mixture to a bowl and let cool.
7. Add cream cheese and mix well.
8. Scoop mixture into balls and serve. Enjoy!

# 169. Chicken and Dill Bombs

**Time taken:** 35 minutes
(plus 30 minutes chill time)
**Servings:** 12

## Ingredients:

- 1 1/2 cup ground chicken
- 2 tbsp olive oil
- 2 tbsp sour cream
- 3/4 cup cream cheese
- 1 tsp paprika
- 1/2 tbsp onion, minced
- 1/2 tsp garlic, minced
- 1 tbsp fresh dill, chopped
- 1 tbsp fresh lemon juice
- salt and pepper to taste

## Directions:

1. Cook chicken, olive oil, garlic and onion in a non-stick pan until chicken is no longer pink.
2. Add paprika, lemon juice, salt, pepper and dill.
3. Transfer mixture to a bowl and let cool.
4. Add the sour cream and cream cheese and mix well.
5. Chill mixture for 30 minutes.
6. Scoop mixture into balls, serve and enjoy!

---

# 170. Chicken and Cilantro Bombs

**Time taken:** 35 minutes
(plus 30 minutes chill time)
**Servings:** 12

## Ingredients:

- 1 1/2 cup ground chicken
- 2 tbsp olive oil
- 2 tbsp sour cream
- 3/4 cup cream cheese
- 1 tsp paprika
- 1/2 tbsp onion, minced
- 1/2 tsp garlic, minced
- 1 tbsp fresh cilantro, chopped
- 1 tbsp fresh lemon juice
- salt and pepper to taste

## Directions:

1. Cook chicken, olive oil, garlic and onion in a non-stick pan until chicken is no longer pink.
2. Add the paprika, lemon juice, salt and pepper.
3. Transfer mixture to a bowl and let cool.
4. Add the sour cream, cream cheese and cilantro and mix well.
5. Chill for 30 minutes.
6. Scoop mixture into balls, serve and enjoy!

---

# 171. Bacon, Egg and Mushroom Bombs

**Time taken:** 15 minutes
(plus 30 minutes chill time)
**Servings:** 12

## Ingredients:

- 10 bacon strips, cooked until crisp and chopped
- 2 tbsp button mushrooms, minced
- 2 hard-boiled eggs
- 3/4 cup cream cheese
- 1 tsp paprika
- 1/2 tbsp onion, minced
- 1/2 tsp garlic, minced
- 1 tbsp fresh cilantro, chopped
- salt and pepper to taste

## Directions:

1. In a large bowl, mash eggs, mushrooms, onion and garlic together with a fork.
2. Add cilantro, bacon, paprika and cream cheese, season to taste with salt and pepper and mix well.
3. Chill the mixture for 30 minutes.
4. Scoop mixture into balls, serve and enjoy!

# 172. Bacon, Egg and Salami Bombs

**Time taken:** 15 minutes
(plus 30 minutes chill time)
**Servings:** 12

## Ingredients:

- 10 bacon strips, cooked until crisp and chopped
- 2 tbsp minced salami
- 2 hard-boiled eggs
- 3/4 cup cream cheese
- 1 tsp paprika
- 1/2 tbsp onion, minced
- 1/2 tsp garlic, minced
- 1 tbsp fresh cilantro, chopped
- salt and pepper to taste

## Directions:

1. In a large bowl, mash eggs, salami, onions, and garlic together with a fork.
2. Add cilantro, bacon, paprika and cream cheese, season to taste with salt and pepper and mix well.
3. Chill mixture for 30 minutes.
4. Scoop mixture into balls, serve and enjoy!

# 173. Caramel Pecan Fudge Fat Bombs

**Time taken:** 20 minutes
(plus 45 minutes chilling time)
**Servings:** 12

## Ingredients:

- 3 cups pecans
- 1/2 tsp vanilla
- 1/2 tsp ground cinnamon
- 1/4 tsp nutmeg
- 1/4 cup stevia
- 1/2 cup coconut oil
- 1/4 cup caramel, melted

## Directions:

1. Using a food processor, pulse the pecans, vanilla, nutmeg and ground cinnamon.
2. Add stevia and coconut oil and mix well.
3. Transfer mixture to a bowl and chill for 30 minutes in the fridge.
4. Line a baking sheet with parchment paper.
5. Scoop mixture into balls and place on the baking sheet.
6. Drizzle caramel over balls and chill for 15 minutes.
7. Serve and enjoy!

# 174. Walnut Fudge Fat Bombs

**Time taken:** 20 minutes
(plus 45 minutes chilling time)
**Servings:** 12

## Ingredients:

- 3 cups walnuts
- 1/2 tsp vanilla
- 1/2 tsp ground cinnamon
- 1/4 tsp nutmeg
- 1/4 cup stevia
- 1/2 cup coconut oil
- 1/4 cup chocolate chips, melted
- 1/4 cup walnuts, chopped

## Directions:

1. Using a food processor, pulse the walnuts, vanilla, nutmeg and ground cinnamon.
2. Add stevia and coconut oil and mix well.
3. Transfer mixture to a bowl and chill for 30 minutes in the fridge.
4. Line a baking sheet with parchment paper.
5. Scoop mixture into balls and place on the baking sheet.
6. Drizzle balls with chocolate, sprinkle with walnuts and chill for 15 minutes.
7. Serve and enjoy!

# 175. Macadamia Caramel Fat Bombs

**Time taken:** 20 minutes
(plus 45 minutes chilling time)
**Servings:** 12

## Ingredients:

- 3 cups macadamia nuts
- 1/2 tsp vanilla
- 1/2 tsp ground cinnamon
- 1/4 tsp nutmeg
- 1/4 cup stevia
- 1/2 cup coconut oil
- 1/4 cup caramel, melted

## Directions:

1. Using a food processor, pulse the macadamia, vanilla, nutmeg and ground cinnamon.
2. Add stevia and coconut oil and mix well.
3. Transfer mixture to a bowl and chill for 30 minutes in the fridge.
4. Line a baking sheet with parchment paper.
5. Scoop mixture into balls and place on the baking sheet.
6. Drizzle balls with caramel and chill for 15 minutes.
7. Serve and enjoy!

# 176. Mixed Nuts Fat Bombs

**Time taken:** 20 minutes
(plus 45 minutes chilling time)
**Servings:** 12

## Ingredients:

- 1 cup macadamia nuts
- 1 cup walnuts

- 1 cup pistachios
- 1/2 tsp ground cinnamon
- 1/4 tsp nutmeg
- 1 tsp vanilla
- 1/4 cup stevia
- 1/2 cup coconut oil
- 1/4 cup caramel, melted

**Directions:**

1. Using a food processor, pulse the macadamia nuts, walnuts, pistachio, vanilla, nutmeg and ground cinnamon.
2. Mix in stevia and coconut oil.
3. Transfer mixture to a bowl and chill for 30 minutes in the fridge.
4. Line a baking sheet with parchment paper.
5. Scoop mixture into balls and place on the baking sheet.
6. Drizzle balls with caramel and chill for 15 minutes.
7. Serve and enjoy!

# 177. Pistachio Fat Bombs

**Time taken:** 20 minutes
(plus 45 minutes chilling time)
**Servings:** 12

## Ingredients:

- 2 cups pistachios
- 1/2 tsp vanilla
- 1/2 cup cream cheese
- 1/2 tsp ground cinnamon
- 1/4 tsp nutmeg
- 1/4 cup stevia
- 1/2 cup coconut oil
- 1/4 cup caramel, melted

**Directions:**

1. Using a food processor, pulse the pistachios, vanilla, nutmeg and ground cinnamon.
2. Add stevia and coconut oil and mix well.
3. Mix in cream cheese.
4. Transfer mixture to a bowl and chill for 30 minutes in the fridge.
5. Line a baking sheet with parchment paper.
6. Scoop mixture into balls and place on the baking sheet.
7. Drizzle balls with caramel and chill for 15 minutes.
8. Serve and enjoy!

# 178. Cherry Chocolate Fat Bombs

**Time taken:** 20 minutes
(plus 1 hour 10 minutes chilling time)
**Servings:** 12

## Ingredients:

- 1 cup cream cheese
- 1/2 tsp vanilla
- 1/4 cup stevia
- 1/2 cup dried cherries, chopped

- 1/2 cup coconut oil
- 1/4 cup desiccated coconut
- 1/4 cup chocolate chips, melted

## Directions:

1. Using a food processor, mix cream cheese and coconut oil.
2. Mix in vanilla and stevia.
3. Add the cherries and mix well.
4. Chill mixture for 1 hour or until hardened.
5. Scoop mixture into balls and roll in desiccated coconut to coat.
6. Drizzle balls with chocolate and chill for another 10 minutes.
7. Serve and enjoy!

# 179. Cherry, Fig and Chocolate Fat Bombs

**Time taken:** 20 minutes
(plus 1 hour 10 minutes chilling time)
**Servings:** 12

## Ingredients:

- 1 cup cream cheese
- 1/2 tsp vanilla
- 1/4 cup stevia
- 1/2 cup dried cherries, chopped
- 1/2 cup coconut oil
- 1/4 cup desiccated coconut
- 1/4 cup chocolate chips, melted
- 1/8 cup dried figs, chopped

## Directions:

1. Using a food processor, combine the cream cheese and coconut oil.
2. Add vanilla and stevia.
3. Add cherries and mix well.
4. Chill mixture for 1 hour or until hardened.
5. Scoop mixture into balls and roll in desiccated coconut to coat.
6. Drizzle balls with chocolate and sprinkle with figs.
7. Chill balls for another 10 minutes.
8. Serve and enjoy!

# 180. Peach Cheesecake Fat Bombs

**Time taken:** 20 minutes
(plus 30 minutes chilling time)
**Servings:** 12

## Ingredients:

- 3/4 cup fresh peaches, chopped
- 3/4 cup cream cheese, softened
- 1 tbsp heavy cream
- 1/4 cup butter, unsalted, softened
- 2 tbsp stevia
- 1 tbsp vanilla
- 1/4 cup corn flakes

## Directions:

1. Using a stand mixer, cream the butter and cream cheese together.
2. Add stevia, heavy cream, and vanilla and mix until smooth.
3. Add chopped peaches and mix until smooth.
4. Cover bowl with cling wrap and let it sit in the fridge for 30 minutes until hardened.
5. Roll mixture into small balls.
6. Roll balls in corn flakes to coat.
7. Serve and enjoy!

# 181. New York Cheesecake Fat Bombs

**Time taken:** 20 minutes
(plus 30 minutes chilling time)
**Servings:** 12

## Ingredients:

- 3/4 cup cream cheese, softened
- 1 tbsp heavy cream
- 1/4 cup butter, unsalted, softened
- 2 tbsp stevia
- 1 tbsp vanilla
- 1/4 cup crushed graham crackers

## Directions:

1. Using a stand mixer, cream the butter and cream cheese together.
2. Add stevia, heavy cream and vanilla and mix until smooth.
3. Cover bowl with cling wrap and let it sit in the fridge for 30 minutes until hardened.
4. Roll mixture into small balls.
5. Roll balls in crushed graham crackers to coat.
6. Serve and enjoy!

# 182. Avocado Cheesecake Fat Bombs

**Time taken:** 20 minutes
(plus 30 minutes chilling time)
**Servings:** 12

## Ingredients:

- 3/4 cup mashed avocado
- 3/4 cup cream cheese, softened
- 1 tbsp heavy cream
- 1/4 cup butter, unsalted, softened
- 2 tbsp stevia
- 1 tbsp vanilla
- 1/4 cup crushed graham crackers

## Directions:

1. Using a stand mixer, cream the butter and cream cheese together.
2. Add avocado, stevia, heavy cream, and vanilla and mix until smooth.
3. Cover bowl with cling wrap and let it sit in the fridge for 30 minutes until hardened.
4. Roll mixture into small balls.
5. Roll balls in crushed graham crackers to coat.
6. Serve and enjoy!

# 183. Mango Cheesecake Fat Bombs

**Time taken:** 20 minutes
(plus 30 minutes chilling time)
**Servings:** 12

## Ingredients:

- 3/4 cup mango, chopped
- 1 tbsp mango puree
- 3/4 cup cream cheese, softened
- 1 tbsp heavy cream
- 1/4 cup butter, unsalted, softened
- 2 tbsp stevia
- 1 tbsp vanilla
- 1/4 cup crushed graham crackers

## Directions:

1. Using a stand mixer, cream butter and cream cheese together.
2. Add mango, mango puree, stevia, heavy cream and vanilla and mix until smooth.
3. Cover bowl with cling wrap and let it sit in the fridge for 30 minutes until hardened.
4. Roll mixture into small balls.
5. Roll balls in crushed graham crackers to coat.
6. Serve and enjoy!

# 184. Green Tea Cheesecake Fat Bombs

**Time taken:** 20 minutes
(plus 30 minutes chilling time)
**Servings:** 12

## Ingredients:

- 3/4 cup cream cheese, softened
- 1 tbsp heavy cream
- 1/4 cup butter, unsalted, softened
- 2 tbsp stevia
- 2 tsp matcha green tea
- 1 tbsp vanilla
- 1/4 cup crushed graham crackers

## Directions:

1. Using a stand mixer, cream the butter and cream cheese together.
2. Add the matcha green tea, stevia, heavy cream and vanilla and mix until smooth.
3. Cover bowl with cling wrap and let it sit in the fridge for 30 minutes until hardened.
4. Roll mixture into small balls.
5. Roll balls in crushed graham crackers to coat.
6. Serve and enjoy!

# 185. Pineapple Cheesecake Fat Bombs

**Time taken:** 20 minutes
(plus 30 minutes chilling time)
**Servings:** 12

## Ingredients:

- 3/4 cup cream cheese, softened
- 2 tbsp heavy cream
- 1/4 cup butter, unsalted, softened
- 2 tbsp stevia
- 1/2 cup pineapple, pureed
- 1 tbsp vanilla
- 1/4 cup crushed graham crackers

**Directions:**

1. Using a stand mixer, cream the butter and cream cheese together.
2. Add the pureed pineapple, stevia, heavy cream, and vanilla and mix until smooth.
3. Cover bowl with cling wrap and let it sit in the fridge for 30 minutes until hardened.
4. Roll mixture into small balls.
5. Roll balls in crushed graham crackers to coat.
6. Serve and enjoy!

# 186. Key Lime Cheesecake Fat Bombs

**Time taken:** 20 minutes
(plus 30 minutes chilling time)
**Servings:** 12

## Ingredients:

- 3/4 cup cream cheese, softened
- 2 tbsp heavy cream
- 1/4 cup butter, unsalted softened
- 2 tbsp stevia
- 1 tbsp lime juice
- 1 tbsp lime zest
- 1 tbsp vanilla
- 1/4 cup crushed graham crackers

## Directions:

1. Using a stand mixer, cream the butter and cream cheese together.
2. Add the lime juice, lime zest, stevia, heavy cream and vanilla and mix until smooth.
3. Cover bowl with cling wrap and let it sit in the fridge for 30 minutes until hardened.
4. Roll mixture into small balls.
5. Roll balls in crushed graham crackers to coat.
6. Serve and enjoy!

# 187. Mango Peach Cheesecake Fat Bombs

**Time taken:** 20 minutes
(plus 30 minutes chilling time)
**Servings:** 12

## Ingredients:

- 3/4 cup cream cheese, softened
- 2 tbsp heavy cream
- 1/4 cup butter, unsalted, softened
- 2 tbsp stevia
- 1/2 cup mango, chopped
- 1/2 cup peaches, sliced
- 1 tbsp vanilla
- 1/4 cup crushed graham crackers

## Directions:

1. Using a stand mixer, cream the butter and cream cheese together.
2. Add peaches, mango, stevia, heavy cream, and vanilla and mix until smooth.
3. Cover bowl with cling wrap and let it sit in the fridge for 30 minutes until hardened.
4. Roll mixture into small balls.
5. Roll balls in crushed graham crackers to coat.
6. Serve and enjoy!

# 188. Frozen Yogurt Cream Fat Bombs

**Time taken:** 20 minutes
(plus 2 hours 20 minutes chilling time)
**Servings:** 12

## Ingredients:

- 2 tbsp heavy cream
- 1 cup dark chocolate chips, melted
- 2 tbsp walnuts, crushed
- 2 cups low-fat yogurt

## Directions:

1. Line a 6x6x2 baking pan with parchment paper.
2. Pour yogurt into pan and freeze for two hours until stiff.
3. Line a baking sheet with parchment paper.
4. In a large bowl, mix the melted chocolate chips, heavy cream and crushed walnuts.
5. Remove yogurt from pan and cut into small 2x2 inch squares.
6. Dip yogurt squares in chocolate to coat and place on the baking tray.
7. Freeze for 20 minutes, serve and enjoy!

# 189. Frozen Strawberry Yogurt Cream Fat Bombs

**Time taken:** 20 minutes
(plus 2 hours 20 minutes chilling time)
**Servings:** 12

## Ingredients:

- 2 tbsp heavy cream
- 1 cup dark chocolate chips, melted
- 2 tbsp walnuts, crushed
- 2 cups low-fat yogurt
- 1 cup strawberries, diced

## Directions:

1. Line a 6x6x2 baking pan with parchment paper.
2. Mix strawberries into yogurt.
3. Pour yogurt mixture into pan and freeze for two hours until stiff.
4. Line a baking sheet with parchment paper.
5. In a large bowl, mix the melted chocolate chips, heavy cream and crushed walnuts.
6. Remove yogurt from pan and cut into small 2x2 inch squares.
7. Dip yogurt squares in chocolate to coat and place on the baking tray.
8. Freeze for 20 minutes, serve and enjoy!

# 190. Frozen Mango Yogurt Cream Fat Bombs

**Time taken:** 20 minutes
(plus 2 hours 20 minutes chilling time)
**Servings:** 12

## Ingredients:

- 2 tbsp heavy cream

- 1 cup dark chocolate chips, melted
- 2 tbs walnuts, crushed
- 2 cups low-fat yogurt
- 1 cup mango, diced

## Directions:

1. Line a 6x6x2 baking pan with parchment paper.
2. Mix mango into yogurt.
3. Pour yogurt mixture into pan and freeze for two hours until stiff.
4. Line a baking sheet with parchment paper.
5. In a large bowl, mix the melted chocolate chips, heavy cream and crushed walnuts.
6. Remove yogurt from pan and cut into small 2x2 inch squares.
7. Dip yogurt squares in chocolate to coat and place on the baking tray.
8. Freeze for 20 minutes, serve and enjoy!

# 191. Frozen Mango Mint Yogurt Cream Fat Bombs

**Time taken:** 20 minutes
(plus 2 hours 20 minutes chilling time)
**Servings:** 12

## Ingredients:

- 2 tbsp heavy cream
- 1 cup dark chocolate chips, melted
- 2 tbs pistachios, crushed
- 2 cups low-fat yogurt
- 1 cup mango, diced
- 1 tsp peppermint oil
- 1 tsp fresh mint, chopped

## Directions:

1. Line a 6x6x2 baking pan with parchment paper.
2. Mix yogurt, mango, peppermint oil and mint.
3. Pour yogurt mixture into baking pan and freeze for two hours until stiff.
4. In a large bowl, mix the melted chocolate chips, heavy cream and crushed pistachios.
5. Line a baking sheet with parchment paper.
6. Remove yogurt from pan and cut into small 2x2 inch squares.
7. Dip yogurt squares in chocolate mixture to coat and place on the baking tray.
8. Freeze for 20 minutes, serve and enjoy!

# 192. Frozen Blueberry Yogurt Cream Fat Bombs

**Time taken:** 20 minutes
(plus 2 hours 20 minutes chilling time)

**Servings:** 12

## Ingredients:

- 2 tbsp heavy cream
- 1 cup dark chocolate chips, melted
- 2 tbs macadamia nuts, crushed
- 2 cups low-fat yogurt
- 1 cup blueberries, diced

## Directions:

1. Line a 6x6x2 baking pan with parchment paper.
2. Mix yogurt and blueberries.
3. Pour yogurt mixture into baking pan and freeze for two hours until stiff.
4. In a large bowl, mix the melted chocolate chips, heavy cream and crushed macadamia nuts.
5. Line a baking sheet with parchment paper.
6. Remove yogurt from pan and cut into small 2x2 inch squares.
7. Dip yogurt squares in chocolate mixture to coat and place on the baking tray.
8. Freeze for 20 minutes, serve and enjoy!

---

# 193. Cinnamon and Coconut Bites

**Time taken:** 20 minutes
(plus 1 hour 30 minutes chilling time)
**Servings:** 12

## Ingredients:

- 1 cup coconut shreds
- 1 tsp stevia powder extract
- 1/2 tsp cinnamon
- 1/2 tsp nutmeg
- 1 tsp vanilla extract
- 1 cup coconut milk
- 1 cup coconut butter

## Directions:

1. Place a glass bowl on top of a saucepan which contains 2 inches of water for the purpose of making a double boiler.
2. Add the coconut butter, coconut milk, vanilla extract, nutmeg, cinnamon and stevia powder to the double boiler and place the double boiler on the stove over a burner on medium heat.
3. Mix the ingredients well as they melt.
4. Once the ingredients are well combined, remove the bowl from the top of the pan and set it in the refrigerator to cool for 30 minutes.
5. Roll the contents of the bowl into balls that are approximately one inch in diameter and then roll them in the shredded coconut to coat.
6. Refrigerate for an additional hour prior to serving.

# 194. Pecan Maple Bites

**Time Taken:** 35 minutes
(plus 1 hour chilling time)
**Servings:** 6

## Ingredients:

Bites Ingredients
- 1/4 tsp liquid stevia
- 1/2 cup coconut oil
- 1/2 cup shredded coconut
- 1/2 cup golden flaxseed meal
- 1 cup almond flour
- 2 cups pecan halves

Syrup Ingredients
- 1/2 tsp cinnamon
- 1/4 tsp xanthan gum
- 1/2 tsp vanilla extract
- 2 tsp maple extract
- 2 1/4 tsp coconut oil
- 1 tbsp unsalted butter
- 1/4 cup powdered erythritol
- 3/4 cups water

## Directions:

Syrup Directions
1. Combine the xanthan gum, butter and coconut oil together in a microwaveable container and mix well.
2. Microwave the container for 40 seconds.
3. Combine the erythritol and cinnamon together in a spice grinder and mix well.
4. Combine the mixture and 3/4 cup of water in a small bowl. Add in the vanilla and maple extracts and mix well.
5. Microwave for 40 seconds, stir well and cool prior to use.
6. This recipe makes 1 cup of liquid.

Bites Directions
1. Start by making sure your oven is heated to 175C/350F.
2. Add the pecan halves to a baking tray that has been covered in tinfoil and let them bake for 6 minutes.
3. Place the pecan halves into a sealable plastic bag and crush them with the help of a rolling pin.
4. Combine the shredded coconut, flaxseed meal and almond flour together using a mixing bowl before mixing in the crushed pecans.
5. Add in the liquid stevia, maple syrup and coconut oil and mix until the results form dough.
6. Add the dough to a casserole dish and place the dish in the oven to let it cook for 20 minutes.
7. Refrigerate for 60 minutes, cut into 12 slices, serve and enjoy.

# 195. Vanilla Fudge

**Time Taken:** 15 minutes
(plus 1 hour chilling time)
**Servings:** 12

## Ingredients:

Fudge Ingredients
- 1/2 vanilla bean pod
- 1 tsp maple extract
- 1/2 cup coconut oil
- 1/2 cup raw butter

Syrup Ingredients
- 1/2 tsp cinnamon
- 1/4 tsp xanthan gum
- 1/2 tsp vanilla extract
- 2 tsp maple extract
- 2 1/4 tsp coconut oil
- 1 tbsp unsalted butter
- 1/4 cup powdered erythritol
- 3/4 cup water

## Directions:

Syrup Instructions
1. Combine the xanthan gum, butter and coconut oil together in a microwaveable container and mix well.
2. Microwave the container for 40 seconds.
3. Combine the erythritol and cinnamon together in a spice grinder and mix well.
4. Combine the mixture and 3/4 cup of water in a small bowl. Add in the vanilla and maple extracts and mix well.
5. Microwave for 40 seconds, stir well and cool prior to use.
6. This recipe makes 1 cup of liquid.

Fudge Instructions
1. Melt the coconut oil as well as the butter.
2. Mix all of the ingredients together in a blender and blend well.
3. Add the results to a glass baking dish, and place in the refrigerator to harden and cool.

# 196. Lemon Drops

**Time Taken:** 5 minutes
(plus 1 hour chilling time)
**Servings:** 12

## Ingredients:

- 1 pinch pink Himalayan salt
- 15 drops liquid stevia
- 2 lemons
- 3 tbsp coconut butter, softened
- 1/4 cup coconut oil, softened

## Directions:

1. Zest both lemons with a microplane utensil.
2. Combine the lemon zest and all of the other ingredients together in a bowl and mix well.
3. Add the results to 12 muffin cups and place them on a tray before setting the tray in the refrigerator for 60 minutes.
4. Refrigerate prior to serving.

# 197. Cinnamon Bun Bars

**Time Taken:** 15 minutes
(plus 2 hours chilling time)
**Servings:** 2

## Ingredients:

- 2 tbsp almond butter
- 1 tbsp coconut oil
- 3/4 tsp cinnamon
- 1/2 cup creamed coconut, in chunks

## Directions:

1. Line a baking dish with muffin liners.
2. Combine the cinnamon and coconut cream in a bowl before adding the results to the dish
3. In a separate bowl, combine 1/4 tsp of coconut oil as well as 1 tbsp of almond butter.
4. Add the results to the baking dish and freeze for 2 hours or until solid.
5. Top the bun bars with 1 tbsp of almond butter and 1/2 tsp of cinnamon.
6. Serve and enjoy!

# 198. Peppermint Patty

**Time Taken:** 10 minutes
(plus 1 hour chilling time)
**Servings:** 6

## Ingredients:

- 4 1/2 oz. coconut oil, melted
- 2 tbsp cocoa powder
- 1/4 tsp peppermint essence
- 1 tbsp granulated stevia

## Directions:

1. Combine the peppermint essence, stevia and coconut oil together in a small bowl and mix well.
2. Add 50 percent of the results to your mold of choice and place in the refrigerator to set, this will form the bottom layer of the patty.
3. Add in the cocoa powder to the remaining mixture and combine well. Add the chocolate layer to the molds once the bottom layer has set, this should take about 30 minutes.
4. Return the molds to the refrigerator and let them set for an additional 30 minutes.

# 199. Pumpkin Fat Bombs

**Time Taken:** 20 minutes
(plus 1 hour chilling time)
**Servings:** 15

## Ingredients:

- 1/2 cup coconut oil, melted
- 1/2 cup pecans, crushed
- 2 tsp pumpkin pie spice

- 1/4 cup erythritol
- 3 tbsp coconut butter, softened
- 1/2 cup pumpkin puree

## Directions:

1. Mix the coconut oil, coconut butter and pumpkin puree together in a mixing bowl before adding in the pumpkin pie spice as well as the erythritol while combining thoroughly.
2. Add the results to your mold of choice and place the mold in the refrigerator for at least 1 hour to allow the bombs to set.
3. While the bombs are cooling, add the pecans to a dry pan before adding the pan to the stove over a burner turned to a medium heat and letting them toast for a few minutes to maximize their flavor.
4. Top each bomb with a few pieces of pecan prior to serving.

## 200. Blackberry Bites

**Time Taken:** 10 minutes
(plus 1 hour chilling time)
**Servings:** 16

## Ingredients:

- 1 cup coconut oil, melted
- 1 tbsp lemon juice
- 1/2 tsp vanilla extract
- 1/2 tsp stevia drops
- 1/2 cup blackberries
- 1 cup coconut butter, softened

## Directions:

1. In a mixing bowl, combine the blackberries, coconut oil and coconut butter and mix well.
2. Add in the remaining ingredients before mixing well and adding the results to a food processor.
3. Mold the mixture into 16 little balls and place these on a pan covered in parchment paper.
4. Add the pan to the refrigerator and let it harden for at least 1 hour prior to serving.

## 201. Frozen Pomegranate Yogurt Cream Fat Bombs

**Time taken:** 20 minutes
(plus 2 hours 20 minutes chilling time)
**Servings:** 12 pieces

## Ingredients:

- 2 tbsp heavy cream
- 1 cup dark chocolate chips, melted
- 2 tbs macadamia, crushed
- 2 cups low-fat yogurt
- 1/2 cup pomegranate puree

## Directions:

1. Line a 6x6x2 baking pan with parchment paper.
2. Mix yogurt and pomegranate puree.
3. Pour yogurt mixture into baking pan and freeze for two hours until stiff.
4. In a large bowl, mix the melted chocolate chips, heavy cream and crushed macadamia nuts.
5. Line a baking sheet with parchment paper.
6. Remove yogurt from pan and cut into small 2x2 inch squares.
7. Dip yogurt squares in the chocolate mixture to coat and place on the baking tray.
8. Freeze for 20 minutes, serve and enjoy!

---

# 202. Frozen Cantaloupe Yogurt Cream Fat Bombs

**Time taken:** 20 minutes
(plus 2 hours 20 minutes chilling time)
**Servings:** 12 pieces

## Ingredients:

- 2 tbsp heavy cream
- 1 cup dark chocolate chips, melted
- 2 tbs macadamia nuts, crushed
- 2 cups low-fat yogurt
- 1 cup cantaloupe, pureed
- 2 tsp melon flavoring

## Directions:

1. Line a 6x6x2 baking pan with parchment paper.
2. Mix yogurt, cantaloupe puree and melon flavoring.
3. Pour yogurt mixture into baking pan and freeze for two hours until stiff.
4. In a large bowl, mix the melted chocolate chips, heavy cream and crushed macadamia nuts.
5. Line a baking sheet with parchment paper.
6. Remove yogurt from pan and cut into small 2x2 inch squares.
7. Dip yogurt squares in the chocolate mixture to coat and place on the baking tray.
8. Freeze for 20 minutes, serve and enjoy!

---

# 203. Cocoa and Nut Fat Bombs

**Time taken:** 10 minutes
(plus 2 hours chilling time)
**Servings:** 12 pieces

## Ingredients:

- 1 cup coconut milk
- 3 tbsp instant gelatin
- 1 tsp vanilla
- 3 tsp cocoa powder
- 1 tsp Himalayan pink salt
- 1 tbsp stevia

## Directions:

1. Using a food processor, blend coconut milk, vanilla, cocoa powder and salt.
2. Add the instant gelatin and stevia.
3. Pour the mixture into an ice cube tray or silicone candy mold.
4. Freeze for 2 hours until hardened.
5. Serve and enjoy!

# 204. Cocoa Caramel Fat Bombs

**Time taken:** 10 minutes
(plus 2 hours 15 minutes chilling time)
**Servings:** 12pcs

## Ingredients:

- 1 cup coconut milk
- 3 tbsp instant gelatin
- 1 tsp vanilla
- 3 tsp cocoa powder
- 1 tsp Himalayan pink salt
- 1 tbsp stevia
- 1/2 cup caramel

## Directions:

1. Using a food processor, blend coconut milk, vanilla, cocoa powder and salt.
2. Add the instant gelatin and stevia.
3. Pour caramel into an ice cube tray or silicone candy mold and chill for 15 minutes.
4. Pour chocolate mixture over caramel and freeze for 2 hours until hardened.
5. Serve and enjoy!

# 205. Macadamia Fat Bombs

**Time taken:** 15 minutes
(plus 2 hours chilling time)
**Servings:** 12 pieces

## Ingredients:

- 2 cups coconut oil, softened
- 1 cup almond butter, softened
- 1/2 cup coconut milk
- 1/2 cup butter, unsalted, softened
- 1 tsp vanilla
- 2 tsp cinnamon
- 1 tsp almond extract
- 1/2 cup macadamia nuts, chopped

## Directions:

1. Using a stand mixer and paddle attachment, cream the coconut oil, almond butter and butter.
2. Slowly add in the coconut milk, vanilla and almond extract
3. Add cinnamon and blend until mixture is smooth.
4. Line a 9x9x2 baking pan with parchment paper and grease the paper.
5. Pour mixture into pan and sprinkle with macadamia nuts.
6. Freeze for 2 hours until hardened.
7. Remove from the pan and cut into 12 equal slices.
8. Serve and enjoy!

# 206. Vanilla Oreo Fat Bombs

**Time taken:** 15 minutes
(plus 2 hours chilling time)
**Servings:** 12 pieces

## Ingredients:

- 2 cups coconut oil, softened
- 2 cups butter, unsalted, softened
- 1/4 cup heavy cream
- 2 tsp vanilla
- 2 tsp cinnamon
- 1/4 cup Oreo cookies, chopped

## Directions:

1. Using a stand mixer and paddle attachment, cream the coconut oil and butter.
2. Slowly add in the heavy cream and vanilla.
3. Add cinnamon and blend until mixture is smooth.
4. Line a 9x9x2 baking pan with parchment paper and grease the paper.
5. Pour mixture into pan and sprinkle with Oreo cookies.
6. Freeze for 2 hours until hardened.
7. Remove from pan and cut into 12 equal slices.
8. Serve and enjoy!

# 207. Peanut Butter and Macadamia Fat Bombs

**Time taken:** 15 minutes
(plus 2 hours chilling time)
**Servings:** 12 pieces

## Ingredients:

- 2 cups coconut oil, softened
- 1 cup almond butter, softened
- 1/2 cup peanut butter
- 1/2 cup butter, unsalted, softened
- 1 tsp vanilla
- 2 tsp cinnamon
- 1/2 cup macadamia nuts, chopped

## Directions:

1. Using a stand mixer and paddle attachment, cream the coconut oil, almond butter and butter.
2. Slowly add in the peanut butter and vanilla.
3. Add cinnamon and blend until mixture is smooth.
4. Line a 9x9x2 baking pan with parchment paper and grease the paper.
5. Pour mixture into pan and sprinkle with macadamia nuts.
6. Freeze for 2 hours until hardened.
7. Remove from the pan and cut into 12 equal slices.
8. Serve and enjoy!

# 208. Vanilla Nut Fat Bombs

**Time taken:** 15 minutes
(plus 2 hours chilling time)

**Servings:** 12 pieces

## Ingredients:

- 2 cups coconut oil, softened
- 1/2 cup butter, unsalted, softened
- 1/4 cup heavy cream
- 2 tsp vanilla
- 2 tsp cinnamon
- 1/4 cup walnuts, chopped
- 1/4 cup almond flakes

## Directions:

1. Using a stand mixer and paddle attachment, cream the coconut oil and butter.
2. Slowly add in the heavy cream and vanilla.
3. Add cinnamon and blend until mixture is smooth.
4. Line a 9x9x2 baking pan with parchment paper and grease the paper.
5. Pour mixture into pan and sprinkle walnuts and almond flakes on top.
6. Freeze for 2 hours until hardened.
7. Remove from the pan and cut into 12 equal slices.
8. Serve and enjoy!

# 209. Vanilla Caramel Fat Bombs

**Time taken:** 15 minutes
(plus 2 hours 15 minutes chilling time)
**Servings:** 12 pieces

## Ingredients:

- 2 cups coconut oil, softened
- 1/2 cup butter, unsalted, softened
- 1/4 cup heavy cream
- 2 tsp vanilla
- 2 tsp cinnamon
- 1 cup caramel, melted

## Directions:

1. Using a stand mixer and paddle attachment, cream the coconut oil and butter.
2. Slowly add in the heavy cream and vanilla.
3. Add cinnamon and blend until mixture is smooth.
4. Line a 9x9x2 baking pan with parchment paper and grease the paper.
5. Pour mixture into pan and chill for 15 minutes.
6. Pour caramel on top and freeze for 2 hours until hardened.
7. Remove from the pan and cut into 12 equal slices.
8. Serve and enjoy!

# 210. Cocoa Vanilla Fat Bombs

**Time taken:** 15 minutes
(plus 2 hours 15 minutes chilling time)
**Servings:** 12 pieces

## Ingredients:

- 2 cups coconut oil, softened
- 1/2 cup butter, unsalted, softened
- 1/4 cup heavy cream
- 2 tsp vanilla
- 2 tsp cinnamon
- 1 cup dark chocolate chips, melted

## Directions:

1. Using a stand mixer and paddle attachment, cream the coconut oil and butter.
2. Slowly add in the heavy cream and vanilla.
3. Add cinnamon and blend until mixture is smooth.
4. Line a 9x9x2 baking pan with parchment paper and grease the paper.
5. Pour mixture into pan and chill for 15 minutes.
6. Pour chocolate on top and freeze for 2 hours until hardened.
7. Remove from the pan and cut into 12 equal slices.
8. Serve and enjoy!

# 211. Almond Butter Fat Bombs

**Time taken:** 15 minutes
(plus 2 hours chilling time)
**Servings:** 8 pieces

## Ingredients:

- 1/2 cup coconut oil, softened
- 1/2 cup almond butter, unsalted, softened
- 1/4 cup butter, unsalted, softened
- 1/4 cup heavy cream
- 2 tsp vanilla
- 1/2 cup almonds
- 1/2 tsp cinnamon
- 1/2 cup white chocolate chips, melted

## Directions:

1. Using a stand mixer and paddle attachment, cream the coconut oil and butter.
2. Slowly add in the heavy cream and vanilla.
3. Add cinnamon and blend until mixture is smooth.
4. Fold in the white chocolate.
5. Line a non-stick mini muffin pan with wax paper cup liners.
6. Place 2-3 almonds in each cup.
7. Pour in the mixture.
8. Freeze for 2 hours until hardened.
9. Remove from the pan, serve and enjoy!

# 212. Spiced Butter Fat Bombs

**Time taken:** 15 minutes
(plus 2 hours chilling time)
**Servings:** 8 pieces

## Ingredients:

- 1/2 cup coconut oil, softened
- 1/2 cup almond butter, unsalted, softened
- 1/4 butter, unsalted, softened
- 1/4 cup heavy cream
- 2 tsp vanilla
- 1/2 cup almonds
- 1/2 tsp cinnamon
- 1/4 tsp cayenne pepper
- 1/4 tsp chili powder
- 1/4 tsp nutmeg
- 1/2 cup white chocolate, melted

## Directions:

1. Using a stand mixer and paddle attachment, cream the coconut oil and butter.
2. Slowly add in the heavy cream and vanilla.
3. Add cinnamon, cayenne pepper, chili powder and nutmeg and blend until mixture is smooth.
4. Fold in the white chocolate.
5. Line a non-stick mini muffin pan with wax paper cup liners.
6. Place 2-3 almonds in each cup.
7. Pour in the mixture and freeze for 2 hours until hardened.
8. Remove from the pan, serve and enjoy!

# 213. Salted Caramel Fat Bombs

**Time taken:** 15 minutes
(plus 2 hours 20 minutes chilling time)
**Servings:** 8 pieces

## Ingredients:

- 1/2 cup coconut oil, softened
- 1/2 cup almond butter, unsalted, softened
- 1/4 butter, unsalted, softened
- 1/4 cup heavy cream
- 2 tsp vanilla
- 1/2 cup almonds
- 1/2 tsp cinnamon
- 1/2 cup white chocolate chips, melted
- 1/2 cup salted caramel chips, melted

## Directions:

1. Using a stand mixer and paddle attachment, cream the coconut oil and butter.
2. Slowly add in the heavy cream and vanilla.
3. Add cinnamon and blend until mixture is smooth.
4. Fold in the white chocolate.
5. Line a non-stick mini muffin pan with wax paper cup liners.
6. Place 2-3 almonds in each cup.
7. Pour in mixture to fill cups 3/4 full.
8. Chill for 20 minutes.
9. Remove from the fridge and pour the salted caramel on top.
10. Freeze for 2 hours until hardened.
11. Remove from the pan, serve and enjoy!

# 214. Ginger Cookie Fat Bombs

**Time taken:** 25 minutes
**Servings:** 12 pieces

## Ingredients:

- 1/2 tbsp butter, unsalted, softened
- 1 egg
- 1 tsp vanilla
- 1 1/2 cups almond flour
- 1/4 cup stevia
- 1 tsp baking soda
- 1/2 cream of tartar
- 1/4 tsp ginger powder
- 1/2 cup brown sugar
- 1/4 tsp cinnamon

## Directions:

1. Preheat oven to 200C/390F.
2. Using a stand mixer and paddle attachment, mix butter, egg and vanilla.
3. Add almond flour, stevia, baking soda, cream of tartar and ginger powder and mix well.
4. Line and baking sheet with parchment paper.
5. Roll dough into 12 balls the size of ping-pong balls.
6. In a small bowl, mix the brown sugar and cinnamon.
7. Roll the dough balls in the cinnamon mixture to coat.
8. Bake cookies for 15-18 minutes.
9. Serve and enjoy!

---

# 215. Cream-filled Cinnamon Fat Bombs

**Time taken:** 25 minutes
**Servings:** 12 pieces

## Ingredients:

- 1/2 tbsp butter, unsalted, softened
- 1 egg
- 1 tsp vanilla
- 1 1/2 cups almond flour
- 1/4 cup stevia
- 1 tsp baking soda
- 1/2 cream of tartar
- 1/4 tsp cinnamon
- 1/2 cup brown sugar
- 12 small cubes cream cheese, frozen

## Directions:

1. Preheat oven to 200C/390F.
2. Using a stand mixer and paddle attachment, mix butter, egg and vanilla.
3. Add almond flour, stevia, cream of tartar and baking soda and mix well.
4. Line a baking sheet with parchment paper.
5. Roll dough into 12 balls the size of ping-pong balls.
6. Stuff a cream cheese cube into each dough ball and roll smooth.
7. In a small bowl, mix the brown sugar and cinnamon.
8. Roll the dough balls in the cinnamon mixture to coat.
9. Bake fat bombs for 15-18 minutes.
10. Serve and enjoy!

# 216. Chocolate-filled Cinnamon Fat Bombs

**Time taken:** 25 minutes
**Servings:** 12 pieces

## Ingredients:

- 1/2 tbsp butter, unsalted, softened
- 1 egg
- 1 tsp vanilla
- 1 1/2 cups almond flour
- 1/4 cup stevia
- 1 tsp baking soda
- 1/2 cream of tartar
- 1/4 tsp cinnamon
- 1/2 cup brown sugar
- 12 small cubes chocolate

## Directions:

1. Preheat oven to 200C/390F.
2. Using a stand mixer and paddle attachment, mix butter, egg and vanilla.
3. Add almond flour, stevia, cream of tartar and baking soda and mix well.
4. Line a baking sheet with parchment paper.
5. Roll dough into 12 balls the size of ping-pong balls.
6. Stuff a piece of chocolate into each dough ball and roll smooth.
7. In a small bowl, mix the brown sugar and cinnamon.
8. Roll the dough balls in the cinnamon mixture to coat.
9. Bake fat bombs for 15-18 minutes.
10. Serve and enjoy!

# 217. Caramel-filled Cinnamon Fat Bombs

**Time taken:** 25 minutes
**Servings:** 12 pieces

## Ingredients:

- 1/2 tbsp butter, unsalted, softened
- 1 egg
- 1 tsp vanilla
- 1 1/2 cups almond flour
- 1/4 cup stevia
- 1 tsp baking soda
- 1/2 cream of tartar
- 1/4 tsp cinnamon
- 1/2 cup brown sugar
- 12 small caramel cubes

## Directions:

1. Preheat oven to 200C/390F.
2. Using a stand mixer and paddle attachment, mix butter, egg and vanilla.
3. Add almond flour, stevia, cream of tartar and baking soda and mix well.
4. Line a baking sheet with parchment paper.
5. Roll dough into 12 balls the size of ping-pong balls.
6. Stuff a caramel cube into each dough ball and roll smooth.
7. In a small bowl, mix the brown sugar and cinnamon.
8. Roll dough balls in the cinnamon mixture to coat.
9. Bake fat bombs for 15-18 minutes.
10. Serve and enjoy!

# 218. Chocolate Chip Fat Bombs

**Time taken:** 25 minutes
**Servings:** 12 pieces

## Ingredients:

- 1/2 tbsp butter, unsalted, softened
- 1 egg
- 1 1/2 cups almond flour
- 1 tsp vanilla
- 1/4 cup stevia
- 1 tsp baking soda
- 1/2 cream of tartar
- 1/4 cup chocolate chips
- 1/4 tsp cinnamon
- 1/2 cup brown sugar

## Directions:

1. Preheat oven to 200C/390F.
2. Using a stand mixer and paddle attachment, mix butter, egg and vanilla.
3. Add almond flour, stevia, cream of tartar and baking soda and mix well.
4. Add in the chocolate chips
5. Line a baking sheet with parchment paper.
6. Roll dough into 12 balls the size of ping-pong balls.
7. In a small bowl, mix the brown sugar and cinnamon.
8. Roll dough balls in the cinnamon mixture to coat.
9. Bake cookie fat bombs for 15-18 minutes.
10. Serve and enjoy!

# 219. Strawberry Cream Fat Bombs

**Time taken:** 15 minutes
(plus 2 hours chilling time)
**Servings:** 12 pieces

## Ingredients:

- 1/4 cup water
- 3/4 cup frozen strawberries
- 1/4 cup protein powder
- 1 cup coconut milk
- 2 tsp stevia

## Directions:

1. Using a high-speed blender, blend strawberries and coconut milk.
2. Add protein powder and water.
3. Add stevia.
4. Line a non-stick mini muffin pan with wax paper cup liners.
5. Pour mixture into muffin pan and freeze for 2 hours.
6. Serve and enjoy!

# 220. Blueberry Cream Fat Bombs

**Time taken:** 15 minutes
(plus 2 hours chilling time)
**Servings:** 12 pieces

- 3/4 cup frozen blueberries
- 1/4 cup protein powder
- 1 cup coconut milk
- 2 tsp stevia

## Ingredients:

- 1/4 cup water

## Directions:

1. Using a high-speed blender, blend blueberries and coconut milk.
2. Add protein powder and water.
3. Add stevia.
4. Line a non-stick mini muffin pan with wax paper cup liners.
5. Pour mixture into muffin pan and freeze for 2 hours.
6. Serve and enjoy!

# 221. Berries and Mint Fat Bombs

**Time taken:** 15 minutes
(plus 2 hours chilling time)
**Servings:** 12pcs

## Ingredients:

- 1/4 cup water
- 1/4 cup frozen blueberries
- 1/4 cup frozen strawberries
- 1/4 cup frozen blackberries
- 1/4 cup protein powder
- 1 cup coconut milk
- 2 tsp stevia
- 1 tsp peppermint oil
- 1 tbsp fresh mint leaves, chopped

## Directions:

1. Using a high speed blender, blend blueberries, strawberries, blackberries and coconut milk.
2. Add protein powder and water.
3. Add stevia and peppermint oil.
4. Add fresh mint leaves
5. Line a non-stick mini muffin pan with wax paper cup liners.
6. Pour mixture into muffin pan and freeze for 2 hours.
7. Serve and enjoy!

# 222. Cinnamon Coconut Bombs

**Time taken:** 10 minutes
(plus 2 hours chilling time)
**Servings:** 10 pieces

## Ingredients:

- 1 cup butter, softened
- 1 tsp cinnamon
- 1 tsp vanilla
- 1 tsp nutmeg
- 1/3 cup coconut shavings

## Directions:

1. In a large bowl, mix butter, cinnamon, vanilla and nutmeg.
2. Chill in the fridge for 30 minutes until mixture hardens a bit.
3. Scoop mixture into balls and roll in coconut shavings to coat.
4. Freeze balls for an hour and a half.
5. Serve and enjoy!

# 223. Spicy Cocoa Walnut Bombs

**Time taken:** 10 minutes
(plus 2 hours chilling time)
**Servings:** 10 pieces

## Ingredients:

- 1 cup butter, softened
- 1 tsp cinnamon
- 1 tsp vanilla
- 1 tsp cayenne pepper
- 1/4 cup walnuts, chopped
- 2 tsp cocoa powder

## Directions:

1. In a large bowl, mix butter, cinnamon and vanilla.
2. Add cayenne pepper and walnuts.
3. Chill in the fridge for 30 minutes until mixture hardens a bit.
4. Scoop mixture into balls and roll in the cocoa powder to coat.
5. Freeze balls for an hour and a half.
6. Serve and enjoy!

# 224. Almond Spice Bombs

**Time taken:** 10 minutes
(plus 2 hours chilling time)
**Servings:** 10 pieces

## Ingredients:

- 1 cup butter, softened
- 1/3 cup almond butter
- 1 tsp cinnamon
- 1 tsp vanilla
- 1 tsp cayenne pepper
- 1/4 cup walnuts, chopped
- 1/2 cup almond flakes

## Directions:

1. In a large bowl, mix butter, almond butter, cinnamon and vanilla.
2. Add cayenne pepper and walnuts.
3. Chill in the fridge for 30 minutes until mixture hardens a bit.
4. Scoop mixture into balls and roll in the almond flakes to coat.
5. Freeze balls for an hour and a half.
6. Serve and enjoy!

# 225. Dill Cilantro Spice Bombs

**Time taken:** 10 minutes
(plus 2 hours chilling time)
**Servings:** 10 pieces

## Ingredients:

- 1 cup butter, softened
- 1/3 cup cream cheese
- 1 tsp vanilla
- 1 tsp fresh dill
- 1 tsp fresh cilantro
- 1/4 cup walnuts, chopped

## Directions:

1. In a large bowl, mix butter, cream cheese and vanilla.
2. Add dill and cilantro.
3. Chill in the fridge for 30 minutes until mixture hardens a bit.
4. Scoop mixture into balls and roll in the walnuts to coat.
5. Freeze balls for an hour and a half.
6. Serve and enjoy!

# 226. Pistachio Sesame Chips

**Time taken:** 1 hour 30 minutes
**Servings:** 10 pieces

## Ingredients:

- 1 1/4 cup sesame seeds
- 1/2 cup sunflower seeds
- 1/8 cup pistachios, chopped
- 1/2 cup water
- 2 eggs
- 1 cup grated cheddar cheese
- 1 tsp Himalayan sea salt

## Directions:

1. Preheat oven to 170C/340F.
2. Line a baking sheet with parchment paper.
3. Mix sesame seeds, sunflower seeds, pistachios, water and eggs.
4. Spread grated cheese over baking sheet.
5. Spread seed mixture over cheese and sprinkle with salt.
6. Bake for 30 minutes.
7. Reduce oven temperature to 140C/285F and bake for 40 more minutes.
8. When cool and dry, break into chips.
9. Serve and enjoy!

# 227. Nutty Sesame Chips

**Time taken:** 1 hour 30 minutes
**Servings:** 10 pieces

## Ingredients:

- 1 1/4 cup sesame seeds
- 1/2 cup walnuts, chopped
- 3/4 cup almond flakes
- 1/2 cup water
- 2 eggs
- 1 cup grated cheddar cheese
- 1 tsp Himalayan sea salt

## Directions:

1. Preheat oven to 170C/340F.
2. Line a baking sheet with parchment paper.
3. Mix sesame seeds, almond flakes, walnuts, water and eggs.
4. Spread grated cheese over the baking sheet.
5. Spread nut mixture over the cheese and sprinkle with salt.
6. Bake for 30 minutes.
7. Lower oven temperature to 140C/285F and bake for 40 more minutes.
8. When cool and dry, break into chips.
9. Serve and enjoy!

# 228. Peppermint Chocolate Bombs

**Time taken:** 15 minutes
(plus 2 hours chilling time)
**Servings:** 10 pieces

## Ingredients:

- 1 avocado, pitted and peeled
- 1 cup coconut milk
- 2 tbsp stevia
- 1 tsp peppermint oil
- 1 cup chopped white chocolate

## Directions:

1. Using a food processor, blend avocado and coconut milk.
2. Add stevia and peppermint oil and pulse until smooth.
3. Mix in the white chocolate.
4. Line a mini muffin pan with wax paper cup liners.
5. Scoop mixture into muffin cups and freeze 2 hours until hardened.
6. Serve and enjoy!

# 229. Strawberry Chocolate Mint Bombs

**Time taken:** 15 minutes
(plus 2 hours chilling time)
**Servings:** 10 pieces

## Ingredients:

- 1/2 cup frozen strawberries
- 1 cup coconut milk
- 2 tbsp stevia
- 1 tsp peppermint oil
- 1 cup chopped white chocolate

## Directions:

1. Using a food processor, blend the strawberries and coconut milk.
2. Add stevia and peppermint oil and pulse until smooth.
3. Mix in the white chocolate.
4. Line a mini muffin pan with wax paper cup liners.
5. Scoop mixture into muffin cups and freeze 2 hours until hardened.
6. Serve and enjoy!

# 230. Blueberry Lime Bombs

**Time taken:** 15 minutes
(plus 2 hours chilling time)
**Servings:** 10 pieces

## Ingredients:

- 1/2 cup frozen blueberries
- 1 cup coconut milk
- 2 tbsp stevia
- 1 tsp lime extract
- 1 cup chopped white chocolate

## Directions:

1. Using a food processor, blend the blueberries and coconut milk.
2. Add stevia and lime extract and pulse until smooth.
3. Mix in the white chocolate.
4. Line a mini muffin pan with wax paper cup liners.
5. Scoop mixture into muffin cups and freeze 2 hours until hardened.
6. Serve and enjoy!

# 231. Lemon Currant Bombs

**Time taken:** 15 minutes
(plus 2 hours chilling time)
**Servings:** 10 pieces

## Ingredients:

- 1/2 cup black currants
- 1 cup coconut milk
- 2 tbsp stevia
- 1 tsp lemon extract
- 1 cup chopped white chocolate

## Directions:

1. Using a food processor, blend the black currants and coconut milk.
2. Add stevia and lemon extract and pulse until smooth.
3. Mix in the white chocolate.
4. Line a mini muffin pan with wax paper cup liners.
5. Scoop mixture into muffin cups and freeze 2 hours until hardened.
6. Serve and enjoy!

# 232. Cherry Coconut Bombs

**Time taken:** 15 minutes
(plus 2 hours chilling time)
**Servings:** 10 pieces

## Ingredients:

- 1/2 cup cherries
- 1 cup coconut milk
- 2 tbsp stevia
- 4 tbsp coconut shavings
- 1 cup chopped white chocolate

## Directions:

1. Using a food processor, blend the cherries and coconut milk.
2. Add stevia and coconut shavings and pulse until smooth.
3. Mix in the white chocolate.
4. Line a mini muffin pan with wax paper cup liners.
5. Scoop mixture into muffin pan and freeze 2 hours until hardened.
6. Serve and enjoy!

# 233. Cilantro Berry Bombs

**Time taken:** 15 minutes
(plus 2 hours chilling time)
**Servings:** 10pcs

- 1/4 cup stevia
- 1/4 cup coconut oil
- 2 tbsp cilantro, chopped

## Ingredients:

- 1 cup strawberries
- 1/2 cup coconut cream
- 3/4 cup cream cheese
- 1 tsp vanilla

## Directions:

1. Using a food processor, blend the strawberries, coconut cream, cream cheese and vanilla.
2. Add stevia, coconut oil and cilantro and pulse until smooth.
3. Line a mini muffin pan with wax paper cup liners.
4. Scoop mixture into muffin pan and freeze 2 hours until hardened.
5. Serve and enjoy!

# 234. Rum Coffee Bombs

**Time taken:** 15 minutes
(plus 2 hours 15 minutes chilling time)
**Servings:** 10 pieces

## Ingredients:

- 1 1/2 cup coconut cream
- 1 tsp cocoa powder
- 2 tsp white rum
- 1/4 cup stevia
- 1/4 cup brewed coffee
- 1 tsp vanilla
- 1 tsp cinnamon
- 1 cup dark chocolate chips, melted

## Directions:

1. Using a food processor, blend the coconut cream, cocoa powder and rum.
2. Add stevia, coffee, cinnamon and vanilla and pulse until smooth.
3. Chill mixture for an hour until hardened.
4. Scoop mixture into balls and freeze for 15 minutes.
5. Coat each ball in melted chocolate and freeze for another hour.
6. Serve and enjoy!

# 235. Chamomile Bombs

**Time taken:** 20 minutes
(plus 3 hour 15 minutes steeping/chilling time)
**Servings:** 10 pieces

## Ingredients:

- 1/2 cup heavy cream
- 2 bags chamomile tea
- 1 cup coconut cream
- 1/4 cup stevia
- 1 tsp honey
- 1 tsp vanilla
- 1 tsp cinnamon
- 1 cup dark chocolate chips, melted

## Directions:

1. Heat heavy cream in a small saucepan.
2. Place chamomile tea bags in heavy cream, cover pan and let steep for 1 hour.
3. Remove and squeeze tea bags and stir cream.
4. Using a food processor, blend heavy cream mixture and coconut cream.
5. Add stevia, honey, cinnamon and vanilla and pulse until smooth.
6. Chill mixture for an hour until hardened.
7. Scoop mixture into balls and freeze for 15 minutes.

8. Coat each ball in melted chocolate and freeze for another hour.

9. Serve and enjoy!

---

# 236. Dark Chocolate Espresso Bombs

**Time taken:** 15 minutes
(plus 2 hours 15 minutes chilling time)
**Servings:** 10 pieces

## Ingredients:

- 1 1/2 cup coconut cream
- 1/4 cup stevia
- 2 tbsp espresso
- 1 tsp cocoa powder
- 1 tsp vanilla
- 1 tsp cinnamon
- 1 cup dark chocolate chips, melted

## Directions:

1. Using a food processor, blend the coconut cream and cocoa powder.
2. Add stevia, espresso, cinnamon and vanilla and pulse until smooth.
3. Chill mixture for an hour until hardened.
4. Scoop mixture into balls and freeze for 15 minutes.
5. Coat each ball in melted chocolate and freeze for another hour.
6. Serve and enjoy!

---

# 237. Espresso Walnut Bombs

**Time taken:** 15 minutes
(plus 2 hours 15 minutes chilling time)
**Servings:** 10 pieces

## Ingredients:

- 1 1/2 cup coconut cream
- 1/4 cup stevia
- 2 tbsp espresso
- 1 tsp cocoa powder
- 1 tsp vanilla
- 1 tsp cinnamon
- 1/2 cup walnuts, chopped
- 1 cup dark chocolate chips, melted

## Directions:

1. Using a food processor, blend the coconut cream and cocoa powder.
2. Add stevia, espresso, cinnamon and vanilla and pulse until smooth.
3. Chill mixture for an hour until hardened.
4. Scoop mixture into balls and freeze for 15 minutes.
5. Coat each ball in melted chocolate and sprinkle with the walnuts.
6. Freeze balls for another hour.
7. Serve and enjoy!

---

# 238. Mojito Bombs

**Time taken:** 15 minutes
(plus 2 hours 15 minutes chilling time)
**Servings:** 10 pieces

## Ingredients:

- 1 1/2 cup coconut cream
- 1/4 cup stevia
- 2 tbsp mojito mix
- 1 tbsp white rum

- 1 tsp lime juice
- 2 tbsp mint leaves
- 1 cup dark chocolate chips, melted

## Directions:

1. Using a food processor, blend coconut cream.
2. Add stevia, mojito mix, rum and lime juice.
3. Add mint leaves and pulse until smooth.
4. Chill mixture for an hour until hardened.
5. Scoop mixture into balls and freeze for 15 minutes.
6. Coat each ball in melted chocolate and freeze for another hour.
7. Serve and enjoy!

# 239. Orange Bombs

**Time taken:** 15 minutes
(plus 2 hours 15 minutes chilling time)
**Servings:** 10 pieces

## Ingredients:

- 1 1/2 cup coconut cream
- 1/4 cup stevia
- 2 tbsp orange puree
- 1 tsp orange zest
- 1 tsp orange extract
- 1 cup dark chocolate chips, melted

## Directions:

1. Using a food processor, blend the coconut cream.
2. Add stevia, orange puree, orange extract, and orange zest and pulse until smooth.
3. Chill mixture for an hour until hardened.
4. Scoop mixture into balls and freeze for 15 minutes.
5. Coat each ball in melted chocolate and freeze for another hour.
6. Serve and enjoy!

# 240. Greek Salad Fat Bombs

**Time taken:** 15 minutes
**Servings:** 12 servings

## Ingredients:

- 1 1/2 cup cream cheese, softened
- 1 cup butter, softened
- 3 tbsp basil, chopped
- 2 garlic cloves, minced
- 1 tbsp cilantro, chopped
- 1 tbsp olives, sliced
- 4 tbsp feta cheese
- salt and pepper to taste

## Directions:

1. In a large bowl, mash cream cheese and butter together with a fork.
2. Add basil, garlic, cilantro and olives.
3. Add salt and pepper to taste and mix well.
4. Scoop mixture into balls and roll in feta cheese.
5. Serve and enjoy!

---

# 241. Artichoke Salad Fat Bombs

**Time taken:** 15 minutes
(plus 1 hour chilling time)
**Servings:** 12 servings

## Ingredients:

- 1 1/2 cups cream cheese, softened
- 1/2 cup sour cream
- 2 tbsp butter, softened
- 1 tsp pepper flakes
- 2 tsp parmesan cheese
- 1 tsp garlic powder
- 1 tbsp onion, minced
- 1 cup artichoke, chopped
- salt and pepper to taste

## Directions:

1. In a large bowl, mash cream cheese with a fork.
2. Add sour cream, butter and pepper flakes and mix well.
3. Add parmesan cheese, garlic powder, onion and artichokes.
4. Add salt and pepper to taste and mix well.
5. Scoop mixture into balls and chill for an hour.
6. Serve and enjoy!

---

# 242. Turkey Blue Cheese Fat Bombs

**Time taken:** 15 minutes
(plus 1 hour chilling time)
**Servings:** 12 servings

## Ingredients:

- 1 1/2 cups cream cheese, softened
- 1/2 cup blue cheese
- 1/4 cup chopped sliced turkey
- 1 tsp mustard
- 2 tbsp celery, minced
- 1 tbsp onion, minced
- salt and pepper to taste

## Directions:

1. In a large bowl, mash cream cheese with a fork.
2. Add blue cheese, turkey, mustard, celery and onion.
3. Add salt and pepper to taste and mix well.
4. Scoop mixture into balls and chill for an hour.
5. Serve and enjoy!

---

# 243. Salmon Blue Cheese Fat Bombs

**Time taken:** 15 minutes
(plus 1 hour chilling time)

**Servings:** 12 servings

## Ingredients:

- 1 1/2 cups cream cheese, softened
- 1/2 cup blue cheese
- 1/4 cup chopped salmon
- 1 tsp lemon juice
- 2 tbsp fresh dill, minced
- 1 tbsp onion, minced
- salt and pepper to taste

## Directions:

1. In a large bowl, mash cream cheese with a fork.
2. Add blue cheese, salmon, lemon juice, dill and onion.
3. Add salt and pepper to taste and mix well.
4. Scoop mixture into balls and chill for an hour.
5. Serve and enjoy!

# 244. Italian Fat Bombs

**Time taken:** 15 minutes
**Servings:** 12 servings

## Ingredients:

- 1 1/2 cup cream cheese, softened
- 1/2 cup fresh mozzarella cheese, grated
- 2 tbsp fresh basil
- 1 tbsp onion, minced
- 1 tbsp olive oil
- 12 small slices of tomato
- 2 tbsp pesto
- salt and pepper to taste

## Directions:

1. In a large bowl, mash cream cheese with a fork.
2. Add mozzarella, basil, onion and olive oil.
3. Add salt and pepper to taste and mix well.
4. Scoop mixture into balls.
5. Set each ball on a tomato slice and top each with a dollop of pesto.
6. Serve and enjoy!

# 245. Mexican Fat Bombs

**Time taken:** 15 minutes
**Servings:** 12 servings

## Ingredients:

- 1 1/2 cup cream cheese, softened
- 1 tbsp Mexican seasoning
- 2 tbsp fresh cilantro
- 1 tsp paprika
- 1 tsp chili flakes
- 1 tsp pickle relish
- 2 tbsp tomatoes, diced
- 1 tbsp onion, minced
- salt and pepper to taste

## Directions:

1. In a large bowl, mash cream cheese with a fork.
2. Add cilantro, paprika, chili flakes, tomatoes, onion, Mexican seasoning and pickle relish.
3. Add salt and pepper to taste and mix well.
4. Scoop mixture into balls, serve and enjoy!

## 246. Bacon Cream Bombs

**Time taken:** 15 minutes
**Servings:** 12 servings

### Ingredients:

- 1 1/2 cup cream cheese, softened
- 2 tbsp heavy cream
- 2 tbsp fresh basil
- 2 tsp garlic, minced
- 1 tbsp onion, minced
- salt and pepper to taste
- 8 slices bacon, cooked until crisp and chopped

### Directions:

1. In a large bowl, mash cream cheese with a fork.
2. Add heavy cream, basil, onion and garlic.
3. Add salt and pepper to taste and mix well.
4. Scoop mixture into balls and roll in the chopped bacon to coat.
5. Serve and enjoy!

## 247. Sun Dried Tomato Bombs

**Time taken:** 15 minutes
**Servings:** 12 servings

### Ingredients:

- 1 1/2 cup cream cheese, softened
- 2 tbsp heavy cream
- 4 tbsp chopped sun dried tomatoes
- 2 tbsp olives, sliced
- 1 tbsp onion, minced
- salt and pepper to taste
- 8 slices bacon, cooked until crisp and chopped

### Directions:

1. In a large bowl, mash cream cheese with a fork.
2. Add heavy cream, sun dried tomatoes, olives and onions.
3. Add salt and pepper to taste and mix well.
4. Scoop mixture into balls and roll in the chopped bacon to coat.
5. Serve and enjoy!

## 248. Cucumber Mint Tomato Bombs

**Time taken:** 15 minutes
**Servings:** 12 servings

### Ingredients:

- 1 1/2 cup cream cheese, softened
- 2 tbsp heavy cream
- 4 tbsp diced cucumber
- 2 tbsp fresh mint, chopped
- 1 tbsp onion, minced
- salt and pepper to taste
- 8 slices bacon, cooked until crisp and chopped

## Directions:

1. In a large bowl, mash cream cheese with a fork.
2. Add heavy cream, cucumber, onion and mint.
3. Add salt and pepper to taste and mix well.
4. Scoop mixture into balls and roll in the chopped bacon to coat.
5. Serve and enjoy!

---

# 249. Dill Sour Cream Bombs

**Time taken:** 15 minutes
**Servings:** 12 servings

## Ingredients:

- 1 1/2 cup cream cheese, softened
- 4 tbsp sour cream
- 4 tbsp diced cheddar cheese
- 2 tbsp fresh dill, chopped
- 1 tbsp onion, minced
- salt and pepper to taste
- 8 slices bacon, cooked until crisp and chopped

## Directions:

1. In a large bowl, mash cream cheese with a fork.
2. Add sour cream, cheddar cheese, onion and dill.
3. Add salt and pepper to taste and mix well.
4. Scoop mixture into balls, and roll the balls into the chopped bacon to coat.
5. Serve and enjoy!

---

# 250. Spiced Avocado Fat Bombs

**Time taken:** 15 minutes
**Servings:** 12 servings

## Ingredients:

- 1 1/2 cup cream cheese, softened
- 4 tbsp heavy cream
- 1/4 cup diced avocado
- 1 tsp cayenne pepper
- 1 tbsp onion, minced
- salt and pepper to taste
- 8 slices bacon, cooked until crisp and chopped

## Directions:

1. In a large bowl, mash cream cheese with a fork.
2. Add heavy cream, avocado, onions and cayenne pepper.
3. Add salt and pepper to taste and mix well.
4. Scoop mixture into balls and roll in the chopped bacon to coat.
5. Serve and enjoy!

# *Dip Recipes*

## 1. Garlic Bacon Cheese Dip

**Time taken:** 40 minutes
**Servings:** 4

### Ingredients:

- 1 cup cream cheese, softened
- 2 cups sour cream
- 1 1/2 cup cheddar cheese, shredded
- 1/2 cup mozzarella, shredded
- 8 slices bacon, cooked until crisp and chopped
- 1/4 cup onion, minced
- 1/2 tbsp garlic, minced
- 1/2 tbsp fresh parsley, chopped
- freshly ground pepper, to taste

### Directions:

1. Preheat oven to 180C/355F.
2. In a large bowl, mash cream cheese and sour cream with a fork.
3. Add onions and garlic and mix well.
4. Spread mixture in a ceramic baking dish.
5. Sprinkle with shredded cheddar cheese and half of the bacon.
6. Sprinkle with mozzarella cheese, remaining bacon, parsley and pepper.
7. Bake for 30 minutes until cheese begins to bubble.
8. Serve dip with fat bombs, veggie sticks, crackers or toasted baguette slices.
9. Enjoy!

## 2. Bacon Avocado Cheese Dip

**Time taken:** 40 minutes
**Servings:** 4

### Ingredients:

- 1 cup cream cheese, softened
- 2 cups sour cream
- 1 avocado, sliced
- 1/2 cup mozzarella, shredded
- 8 slices bacon, cooked until crisp and chopped
- 1/4 cup yellow pepper, minced
- 1/4 cup onion, minced
- 1/2 tbsp garlic, minced
- 1/2 tbsp fresh parsley, chopped
- freshly ground pepper, to taste

## Directions:

1. Preheat oven to 180C/355F.
2. In a large bowl, mash cream cheese and sour cream with a fork.
3. Add onions, yellow pepper and garlic and mix well.
4. Spread mixture in a ceramic baking dish.
5. Arrange avocado slices over mixture.
6. Sprinkle with mozzarella, bacon, parsley and pepper.
7. Bake for 30 minutes until cheese begins to bubble.
8. Serve dip with fat bombs, veggie sticks, crackers or toasted baguette slices.
9. Enjoy!

# 3. Molten 4-Cheese Dip

**Time taken:** 40 minutes
**Servings:** 4

## Ingredients:

- 1 cup cream cheese, softened
- 2 cups sour cream
- 1/2 cup mozzarella, shredded
- 1 1/2 cup cheddar cheese, shredded
- 1 cup feta cheese, crumbled
- 8 slices bacon, cooked until crisp and chopped
- 1/4 cup onion, minced
- 1/2 tbsp garlic, minced
- 1/2 tbsp fresh parsley, chopped
- freshly ground pepper, to taste

## Directions:

1. Preheat oven to 180C/355F.
2. In a large bowl, mash cream cheese and sour cream with a fork.
3. Add onions and garlic and mix well.
4. Spread mixture in a ceramic baking dish.
5. Sprinkle with shredded cheddar cheese and half of the bacon.
6. Sprinkle with mozzarella, remaining bacon, feta cheese, parsley and pepper.
7. Bake for 30 minutes until the cheese begins to bubble.
8. Serve with fat bombs, veggie sticks, crackers or toasted baguette slices.
9. Enjoy!

# 4. Bacon Blue Cheese Dip

**Time taken:** 40 minutes
**Servings:** 4

## Ingredients:

- 1 cup cream cheese, softened
- 2 cups sour cream
- 1 1/2 cup mozzarella, shredded
- 1 cup blue cheese, crumbled
- 8 slice bacon, cooked until crisp and chopped
- 1/4 cup onion, minced
- 1/2 tbsp garlic, minced
- 1/2 tbsp fresh parsley, chopped
- freshly ground pepper, to taste

## Directions:

1. Preheat oven to 180C/355F.
2. In a large bowl, mash cream cheese and sour cream.
3. Add onions and garlic and mix well.
4. Spread mixture in a ceramic baking dish.
5. Sprinkle with blue cheese and half of the bacon.
6. Sprinkle with mozzarella, remaining bacon, parsley and pepper.
7. Bake for 30 minutes until the cheese begins to bubble.
8. Serve with fat bombs, veggie sticks, crackers or toasted baguette slices.
9. Enjoy!

# 5. Bacon and Onion Dip

**Time taken:** 40 minutes
**Servings:** 4

## Ingredients:

- 2 large onions, sliced
- 1/2 cup mozzarella, grated
- 1 cup cream cheese, softened
- 2 cups sour cream
- 10 slices bacon, cooked until crisp and chopped
- 2 tbsp olive oil
- 1/2 tbsp garlic, minced
- 1/2 tbsp fresh parsley, chopped
- freshly ground pepper, to taste

## Directions:

1. Preheat oven to 180C/355F.
2. In a large saucepan, cook onion in olive oil until browned.
3. Transfer onion mixture to a large bowl.
4. Add cream cheese, sour cream, garlic and bacon and mix well.
5. Spread mixture in a ceramic baking dish.
6. Sprinkle with mozzarella, parsley and pepper.
7. Bake for 30 minutes until the cheese begins to bubble.
8. Serve with fat bombs, veggie sticks, crackers or toasted baguette slices.
9. Enjoy!

# 6. Garlic Parmesan Dip

**Time taken:** 40 minutes
**Servings:** 4

## Ingredients:

- 1/2 cup parmesan cheese, grated
- 1 cup cream cheese, softened
- 2 cups sour cream
- 5 slices bacon, cooked until crisp and chopped
- 2 tbsp olive oil
- 1 tsp garlic powder
- 2 tbsp garlic, minced
- 1/2 tbsp fresh parsley, chopped
- freshly ground pepper, to taste

## Directions:

1. Preheat oven to 180C/355F.
2. In a large bowl, mash cream cheese and sour cream with a fork.
3. Add garlic and garlic powder and mix well.
4. Spread mixture in a ceramic baking dish.
5. Sprinkle with parmesan cheese, parsley, bacon and pepper.
6. Bake for 30 minutes until the cheese begins to bubble.
7. Serve with fat bombs, veggie sticks, crackers or toasted baguette slices.
8. Enjoy!

# *Conclusion*

I hope you enjoyed all of the simple, but delicious "Fat Bomb" recipes in this cookbook!

For more ketogenic cookbooks, or other delicious and healthy cookbooks, make sure to check out my author page on Amazon, as I'm constantly creating more cookbooks to accommodate those who wish to live a healthy lifestyle.

If you enjoyed this book and found it helpful, please take the time to leave me a review on Amazon. I appreciate your honest feedback, and it really helps me to continue producing high-quality books.

Simply go to this url to leave a review, https://www.amazon.com/dp/B06X9G472Y/

Made in the USA
San Bernardino, CA
13 August 2017